500

Tips for Tutors

**PHIL RACE AND
SALLY BROWN**

**KOGAN
PAGE**

London • Philadelphia

lucation Series

500 Tips for Tutors Phil Race and Sally Brown
Case Studies on Teaching in Higher Education Peter Schwartz and
  Graham Webb
Using Learning Contracts in Higher Education Edited by Mike Laycock and
  John Stephenson

First published in 1993
Reprinted 1994, 1995, 1997

Kogan Page Limited
120 Pentonville Road
London N1 9JN

British Library Cataloguing in Publication Data

A CIP record for this book is available from the British Library.

ISBN 0 7494 0987 8

Typeset by DP Photosetting, Aylesbury, Bucks
Printed and bound in Great Britain by
Biddles Ltd, Guildford and King's Lynn

Contents

Preface

There are already hundreds of books and papers about good teaching practices. We even know of one which gives fascinating advice on how best to hold a stick of chalk (and much more besides). Here, however, we wanted to forget about teaching and concentrate on learning. If the learning is going well, the teaching must be all right too.

We've written this book for lecturers at universities and colleges. We hope it will be useful not only to new staff, but equally to experienced colleagues. The book is intended to be a dip-in resource for busy tutors, who can pick out particular ideas relevant to the teaching they are immediately engaged in. The book is also intended to be used when planning new courses and when updating existing courses, particularly when it is intended to make major strides towards learner-centred learning. The book will also be of interest to learners, who will find ideas which they can use to help them make the most of the different teaching/learning situations they encounter.

In this book, we've assembled 50 sets of 'Ten Tips'. Each set is intended to be complete in itself, and we've deliberately included some overlaps, as the various ways in which people learn overlap anyway. We don't for a minute pretend that we've covered everything!

We've structured the book into something that very roughly represents 'chronological order', starting with trying to find ways of helping students before they arrive, to helping them set out on their quest for employment. However, apart from this, the chronology is rather futile, since learners will meet such things as lectures, tutorials, seminars and assessment in a fairly random order. We've therefore tried to group together our sets of suggestions into six broad areas:

- general study skills
- starting off and working together
- lectures and written work
- learning resources
- various kinds of assessment
- life skills.

Phil Race, University of Glamorgan, Pontypridd
Sally Brown, University of Northumbria, Newcastle-upon-Tyne

How to use this book

This book contains practical suggestions for ways of helping learners adopt more active approaches to their learning, and develop study-skills and life-skills which will see them safely through their education. It's not so much a 'teaching tips' book; it's more a book of tips on ways of helping people to learn well. We've written it as a 'start anywhere' resource. Among the ways you may find of using it are:

- look for any area where you think your learners have problems
- select one particular idea, and try it out
- see if any of the ideas help you with parts of your work you find difficult
- use any set of 'ten tips' as a discussion-starter with your colleagues
- use particular pages to give learners food for thought or discussion-starters
- think of better ideas and advice (and write to us and share with us).

Remember, we're not trying to tell anyone how to do their job. All we're offering are suggestions. We've written these suggestions very much trying to keep learners themselves to the fore in our minds, and looking for ways that we ourselves as tutors can help them. We hope our suggestions are useful to you too.

We will very much appreciate your comments on our attempt to provide useful suggestions – and will be especially grateful for any additional suggestions you may be willing to offer (and will be pleased to credit you in our next edition).

Part 1

General Study Skills

1 Helping learners prepare to start your course
2 Helping learners explore how they learn
3 Helping learners develop time-management skills
4 Helping learners develop task-management skills
5 Helping learners find the questions
6 Learning more from reading
7 Making time for reflection
8 Helping learners prepare for vivas

In this section, we look at ways that learners can be helped to do some useful preparation before they start your course, then suggest how you can help them explore their own learning strategies. Then we remind you of a selection of general study skills, which can be useful to learners either throughout their studies or on particular occasions.

1

Helping learners prepare to start your course

Before the start of a course or module, there are often vacations or other 'slack time' when learners can, if they wish, do much to pave the way to success. This depends on their knowing what may be useful. Here are some ways to help them.

1   Try to ensure that learners are given printed documentation about your course (or your part of a course) **some time in advance**. A syllabus, for example, can be a useful start.

2   It can be useful to prepare a **pre-reading list**, giving learners some ideas about useful sources to consult before the course begins. The shorter and more focused such a list is, the more likely it is that learners will try to do some pre-reading.

3   Don't just suggest *what* to read, **explain *why* it's useful to read each major piece**, and give positive suggestions regarding what learners should try to extract from each source. Arming learners with lists of questions can be a very productive way of helping them focus their reading.

4   The sooner learners know about **the standards they will eventually need to achieve**, the more they can adjust their expectations of your course. Giving examples of syllabus objectives, relevant assessment criteria, and last year's exam questions can be useful ways of helping learners tune in to the level of your course.

5   **A pre-course learning package** can be a very worthwhile luxury. Although this may take some time for you to put together, it can serve a valuable role in years to come. A useful package will be a mixture of information, references and tasks and activities, with particular attention being given to designing printed *responses* to the tasks and activities, so that learners working alone through the pre-course package have the benefit of feedback on their attempts.

6   Provide learners with a list of **'useful things to do before starting this course'**. Some of these things could be relevant past knowledge to brush up, ideas and thoughts to collect together, maybe even suggestions for a little preliminary experimentation or field work.

7   Advice on **what to bring to the start of the course** is always welcomed by learners. However, they need more than a list of 20 textbooks. They need a 'user-friendly' guide. It can be useful to enlist the help of some learners who have finished the course (successfully) to put together a 'what to get beforehand' checklist.

8   **Drafting a letter to new learners** can be a valuable way of breaking the ice with them. This is particularly relevant when your contribution is at the very start of an entire course. Such letters can have up-to-date information, for example the times and places of the first few components of your part of their course.

9   Don't forget that some of the time just before starting a new course can be usefully spent by learners **appraising their study skills**. It can be useful to recommend one or two useful sources of relevant study skills advice (or better still, write some key suggestions yourself).

10   When sending out ideas for pre-course preparation, ensure that learners **won't feel 'snowed under'** by a mass of paperwork. If it all looks too daunting, they'll probably do none of it – or maybe won't arrive at all. A 'front-sheet' summarizing the bits and pieces in your 'pre-course' pack – and marking several as 'optional' – can help learners take a balanced view of it all.

2

Helping learners explore how they learn

The more learners know about the processes by which they learn best, the more they can harness the processes to their advantage. The following ideas can be used to help people see some key steps in the ways they learn.

1   Ask learners to think of **something they're good at**, and to jot it down.

2   Ask them to write down a few words explaining **how** they became good at whatever it was.

3   **Help them compare their responses to the previous two questions.** For example, most learners will have used words such as 'doing it', 'practice', 'repetition', 'trial and error', 'getting it wrong at first'. Use these ideas to help them see that most learning is done in an active way. Remind them how useful it can be to learn by making mistakes, and how therefore it is useful to regard mistakes as valuable learning experiences.

4   Comment on how **rarely** people declare that they became good at something through 'being taught' or 'being shown how' and so on. From this, draw out the need for learners to take an active part in the teaching/learning situations they encounter, rather than sit passively 'being taught and hoping it will stick'.

5   **Ask learners to think of something they *feel* good about,** for example a personal attribute or quality. Ask them to jot it down. Then ask them to write down a few words explaining upon what basis they feel good about whatever they wrote down in answer to the previous question. In other words, ask them 'upon what evidence do you have this positive feeling?'

6　**Help learners to compare what gives them positive feelings**. By far the most frequent answers include phrases such as 'other people's reactions', 'feedback from other people', 'the expressions on people's faces', 'people come back to me for help' and so on. In other words, the keys to positive feelings tend to be feedback and other people. This can be a useful way of helping learners develop a healthy 'thirst for feedback' rather than trying to hide from situations where other people see how they're doing.

7　**Remind learners that studying is not a completely separate part of their lives.** The same processes that lead to becoming good at anything in life also apply to successful studying. Similarly, the same processes which lead to positive feelings about anything in life also apply to developing positive feelings about studying.

8　**Ask learners to think of some learning experience that went wrong** and to write down a few words about what happened to make it an unsuccessful learning experience.

9　**Help them to compare the causes of poor learning experiences**. Common causes relate to a lack of feedback (therefore lack of positive feelings), and to lack of opportunity to practise (therefore a lack of 'learning by doing'). Other causes are lack of motivation, in other words, no deep wish to succeed, or a lack of time to make sense of it all, or no time to reflect.

10　**Draw out once more the four main requirements for successful (and enjoyable) learning, ie:**

> wanting to learn – motivation, a sense of purpose;
> learning by doing – practising, making mistakes;
> feedback from other people – leading to positive feelings about what has been learned;
> digesting – time to reflect and make sense of what has been learned.

It can be useful to keep reminding learners of the importance of all four of the above as they continue into your course, and helping them work out ways of linking these fundamental learning processes with the content of your course.

3

Helping learners develop time-management skills

The number of hours in each day is given to all people in equal measure, but time-management skills are widely underdeveloped. If we can manage our time well, we can manage just about everything else. The ten suggestions which follow can help learners increase their mastery over time.

1   Help learners to **work out the benefits** of well-developed time-management skills. Help them see that personal productivity, personal efficiency and personal effectiveness are all connected with their ability to manage time. Allow them to work out that time-management skills have life-long value and enhance all their other skills and aptitudes.

2   **Get learners thinking about learning quality**. Ask them what kinds of activity have a high payoff in terms of learning. These can include discussing, explaining, summarizing, problem-solving and quizzing each other. Ask them what kinds of activity have low learning-payoff; these can include writing in copying mode, reading passively, and appearing to listen.

3   **Get learners to stop and reflect on what they have learned**. Ask them to work out how their learning happened, exactly what they learned, when exactly the learning happened, and how it can be made more efficient next time.

4   Show learners how wasteful and miserable **just *thinking* about work** can be – compared with getting on with it. Time spent thinking about work has associations with guilty conscience and looming tasks. Time spent *after* work has been successfully completed is high-quality time – the most enjoyable sort of time.

5   Help learners work out how often 90 per cent of things tend to get done in the last 10 per cent of the time available. Point out that it is therefore logical that most things can be done in the *first* **10 per cent of the time available** – leading to the luxury of much more genuinely 'free' time. Hint at the positive feelings and confidence that come with always having things done well ahead of schedule.

6   **Get learners to set deadlines for themselves**. Encourage them to set several stage deadlines rather than one final deadline. Encourage them to break large tasks into manageable chunks. Encourage them to set deadlines 'early' to allow for the unexpected.

7   Point out the benefit of doing **half-an-hour's work on a non-urgent task** each time before starting an urgent one. The urgent one will still get done, as there is pressure to complete it. The practice of doing a little non-urgent work gradually leads to the situation where there are fewer and fewer urgent tasks. After all, 'urgent' usually is synonymous with 'late'.

8   Conduct a **negative-brainstorm** on time-management with learners. Ask them 'what are the results of *not* being skilled at time-management?', then analyse how these consequences can best be avoided.

9   **Help learners to maximize their use of peer-support**. Get them to use each other in setting and monitoring deadlines. Show them that when more people know about a deadline, it is more likely it will be met.

10   **Give learners the feeling of ownership of time**. No one develops time-management skills under an imposed regime. Give learners time, and the responsibility for making good use of time.

4

Helping learners develop task-management skills

Task-management is at least as important as time-management. The following suggestions can help your learners to sort out the respective priorities of the various tasks which they need to do in the course of their studies.

1   Suggest that each day your learners make a **list of things on their agenda**.

2   **Prioritize the tasks** in terms of five categories: 'must be done today', 'should be done today', 'may be done today', 'could be started today', 'not necessary today'. This can be done, for example, using Post-its for the tasks, and a wallchart. Items can be moved up the wall as they become more urgent. Point out the value of choosing tasks from more than one category on each day. In other words, just doing 'must be done today' tasks does not help to prevent a backlog building up, whereas doing (or starting) one or two low-priority tasks each day has the long-term benefit of preventing an accumulation of urgent tasks.

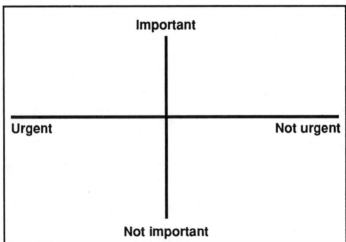

3   Suggest that learners make an **'urgency/importance' grid**, and decide which tasks go in which box.
Then suggest the strategy:

a: do urgent and important things first;
b: do urgent but not important things quickly, not spending too much energy on them;
c: allocate time ahead for important but non-urgent work;
d: try to delegate or drop non-urgent, non-important tasks, or use them as 'spacer-tasks' to break up the boredom of long jobs.

4   Remind learners that a task is usually done **more easily** if it is not really urgent. When something must be completed at once, it tends not to be approached in a relaxed and creative way, and is therefore rarely done really well.

5   Suggest that it may be better to do **three things** on the list today (even without finishing any of them) rather than to spend all the available time on one task.

6   Encourage learners to allocate themselves **rewards** on the completion of tasks (or major stages in a big task).

7   Explain the usefulness of letting **other people** know one's plans. If friends or family are likely to ask 'did you get that task done you were telling me about?' there is a considerable incentive not to be 'caught lacking'. Let your learners know of one of your own projected deadlines for a task.

8   Encourage the use of **stage deadlines**, rather than one final deadline.

9   Suggest the use of **'targets'** as well as 'deadlines'. The deadline is likely to be imposed externally, whereas targets can be self-imposed. The feeling of ownership of targets makes it highly attractive to try to meet them (especially if other people are aware of one's targets).

10   **Set an example.** Show learners your own approaches to managing the various tasks in a typical day or week. Share approaches which are effective – but even better – share your approaches which fail! Learning from other people's mistakes is a particularly attractive way to learn.

5

Helping learners find the questions

'If you know what the questions are, you're more than halfway towards being able to answer them' – how often have we told learners this? However, they often seem to need some help before they make good use of question-devising strategies in their studies.

1   Remind learners that exams essentially will test **their ability to answer questions in writing**. This, like any other skill, can be dramatically improved by practising.

2   Suggest that learners continuously ask themselves **'what may I reasonably be expected to be able to do with this?'** Suggest that they ask themselves this during lectures, while reading, in tutorials, and in every part of their studies. The word 'reasonably' is important – there's no point in them trying to prepare for things that could not be reasonably expected of them (for example learning massive amounts of numerical or statistical data).

3   Encourage learners to make themselves **'question banks'**. Suggest that these should contain large numbers of short, sharp questions, based on what they think may be expected of them. Suggest that when they know how to answer a wide range of short, sharp questions, they will automatically be in a strong position to put together answers to longer, complex questions.

4   **Advise learners to get hold of past exam papers**, early in the course (if they leave them until late, they may find them frightening!). Suggest that they break the exam questions down into shorter, sharper components, and add these to their question banks.

5   Remind learners that becoming able to do things depends **mainly on practice**. Therefore, it is of little value just reading through questions and answers. When an answer is in sight, the eyes will stray straight to it, robbing learners of any real chance to start practising with the question.

6   Remind learners that case-studies, worked examples and problems that are **shown to them in lectures and tutorials** may well be things that they in turn will be expected to be able to do in exams. Therefore, suggest that they add the *questions* from things covered in class to their question banks.

7   Advise learners that things such as essays, homework assignments, tutorial exercises and practical-work questions can all be the basis of similar exam questions. Suggest that they **add all these questions to their question banks**, and use them for practice.

8   Encourage learners to compile question-banks **collaboratively**. A group of learners will quickly build up a more comprehensive question-bank than an individual.

9   Suggest that it's well worth writing down and storing questions, even **before learners know the answers**. If they have the question on file, sooner or later there will be a way of finding out the answer. If the question was not put on file, the question itself would quickly be forgotten.

10 Since practising answering questions is such valuable practice for exams, suggest that learners do it in **as many ways as they can** – written answers 'mental' answers, and oral answers. Working in small groups is a particularly effective way of getting through a lot of question-answering in a short time, for example by learners quizzing each other using a question bank.

6

Learning more from reading

The term 'reading for a degree' has been around for a long time, yet reading is a skill which relatively few learners have developed as systematically as they could. The following suggestions may help learners take more control of their reading styles.

1   **Remind learners how easy it is to read passively**. You could demonstrate this to them in a large-group session by giving them a handout with some printed information, then later in the session testing them on the content. Suggest that time spent 'just reading' can be almost wasted as far as real learning is concerned, and that they can and should develop additional ways of focusing their attention as they read.

2   **Point out the value of jotting down questions *before* reading something**. It then becomes 'reading with an agenda in mind' and is automatically more active. As answers to the questions are found, they tend to register.

3   Remind learners that the most important pages of textbooks are often the **contents pages** and the **index**. Suggest that tracking down the relevant information is one of the most important aspects of good reading skills.

4   Suggest that active reading is normally **done with a pen!** For example, making summary notes or mental maps are useful ways of helping ensure that the important ideas are being 'distilled and refined' during reading.

5   Since the measure of how effectively they have read something depends on how well they can apply it or answer questions on it, suggest that as learners read, they should **jot down questions**. These questions can later serve as triggers for the important information they have been reading about.

6   **Give learners suggestions about when speed-reading can be useful.**
     For example, when doing a preliminary 'skim' of a large body of
     information, speed-reading is very useful for creating a mental map
     of the information available. Suggest that learners check that they are
     not 'stuck' in a 'recitation' mode of reading (often picked up at school
     in reading-aloud exercises) where the speed of reading is limited by
     to the speed at which learners can 'hear' the words in their minds.
     Help them to realize that they can read several times faster than they
     can 'hear'.

7   For some kinds of information, reading just the **first sentence of
     every paragraph** can be enough. This technique is particularly useful
     as part of a process of finding the most relevant paragraphs, which
     can then be read more slowly and completely.

8   Recommend to learners that they **'make their books their own'**, for
     example by writing on them, using highlighter pens, photocopying
     crucial extracts for personal use and arranging them in a scrapbook
     format, and so on. (Obviously, advise against defacing library copies
     – most libraries have photocopying facilities).

9   Advise learners that **quality of reading and relevance** are much more
     important than mere breadth of reading – especially when preparing
     for written exams. Only so much can be written in an exam room.

10   Finally, despite the various ways of improving the quality of reading,
     remind learners that most 'real learning' is **learning-by-doing**, and
     activities such as practising answering questions have a higher
     learning-payoff than reading.

7

Making time for reflection

When you only have a given number of hours to cover your parts of a syllabus with learners, it is all too easy to fill all the available hours with planned teaching. It is important to accommodate learners' need for time to reflect on what they are studying.

1 Keep reminding learners that it is not enough for them simply to be there at lectures, tutorials, laboratory classes and so on. In addition, they need to work out **their own ways** of consolidating what they are learning, doing coursework and preparing for assessment.

2 **Devise short tasks to set learners**, such that they necessarily reflect on material they have been introduced to. Such tasks can be the basis of tutorial and seminar activities.

3 One way of allowing learners to reflect on learning experiences is to ask them to **provide you with feedback about their learning**. Issuing a questionnaire asking them (for example) to categorize various topics into 'completely understand' 'more-or-less understand' 'don't yet understand' gives you feedback about their progress, but also helps them to reflect on their individual positions (and to compare their feelings with colleagues).

4 Explain the importance of **repetition** in learning and understanding. Suggest that it's more useful to go over something for a few minutes several times, than to spend one long spell studying it. Explain that when repeatedly spending a short time studying something, the subconscious mind is continuing to process the information and making sense of it.

5 **Suggest useful reflection techniques to learners**. For example, get them to review a lecture by deciding their answer to a question such as 'if there were just two things I would need to remember from this lecture, they would be (1) ... and (2) ...'.

6   Remind learners of the dangers of reading passively, just turning the pages without any real learning occurring. Suggest that they reflect at frequent intervals on what they have just been reading, for example by making a **short summary or mind-map** of it, or by turning what they have learned into a list of short questions to quiz themselves with later.

7   **Build some reflection-type activities into your teaching sessions.** For example, use a lecture period now and then to pose a series of problems or issues based on material they have met already, getting learners first to reach individual decisions or answers, then leading into a discussion or debriefing with the whole group.

8   When deciding topics for student-led seminars, help to ensure that the **preparation** for the seminars will include reflecting on material that has already been covered in the course and linking it to the specific topics of the seminars.

9   Advise learners that they can use **all sorts of times** to reflect. A considerable amount of reflection can be done in just a few minutes. Odd bits of time that may otherwise be completely wasted can be used for useful reflection – for example, waiting in a queue, train journeys, boring bits of lectures and so on.

10   Enthuse learners with how useful it can be to deliberately reflect **with a few of their peers**. Two or three people looking back at a lecture (or something they have all just read) can come up with more ideas than any one person would have, and because they are explaining their ideas by putting them into words to each other, the ideas will be more firmly registered in their minds, leading to deeper learning.

8

Helping learners prepare for vivas

In some courses, everyone has vivas. In other courses, vivas may only be used at the end, mainly to work out what to do with borderline cases. As with other aspects of study skills, it can pay dividends to help learners prepare constructively for vivas.

1   If vivas are used as a normal part of your course, **explain exactly how much they will count for** and when they will take place.

2   Where vivas are used to help decide what to do with borderline cases, explain that normally a viva means a chance to **move 'up'** rather than to move 'down'. Emphasize, also, that it is then normal to include representative candidates from the 'mid-range' to provide a frame of reference (and that such candidates should certainly not be apprehensive about the fact that they are having a viva).

3   Accept that some learners have an **instinctive fear** of the 'public' sort of scrutiny they may be under in the situation of a viva. They quite naturally may feel intimidated at the prospect of being questioned by one or more experts or 'figures of authority'.

4   Suggest to learners that the skills of doing well in viva situations are worth developing **consciously**. Similar skills will be needed many times during their careers, for example at interviews, promotion boards and so on.

5   Confirm that skills at handling viva situations effectively (like many other practical skills) are **best developed through practice**. Encourage learners to set up their own mock viva panels, and to practise until they feel quite comfortable in the situation of being 'put on the spot'. Postgraduate learners preparing for PhD vivas often spend many weeks practising together in this way.

6   Advise learners that there are particular preparations they can make **in advance** of a viva. They don't have to simply hope that 'it'll be all right on the day'. For example, they can decide what *won't* be expected of them in a viva – things such as lengthy computations or derivations and so on.

7   Remind learners that a viva is essentially a question-and-answer session **and most of the questions will be quite short**. They can therefore prepare for a viva by working out as many likely questions as they can think of and practising giving oral answers to them.

8   When a viva is being used as a second-chance process, it will usually be because something has not worked out well in another part of the assessment scheme – for example, a poorer-than-expected exam performance. It is then quite likely that part of the viva will focus on the exam which went badly. It is therefore useful to advise learners to **check up on things that they know may have gone wrong** in their exams as part of their preparations for a viva.

9   **Help learners to be aware of the need to create a favourable impression.** It can be useful to show a group of learners preparing for vivas some video clips of different behaviours shown by candidates (preferably role-played). Better still, if all the learners are preparing for a similar viva, let them do some role-playing in front of a video camera, then watch themselves.

10   **Caution learners about the dangers of 'waffling'!** Unkind examiners in vivas have been known to allow learners to go in deeper and deeper once they started to invent answers to questions.

Organizing your studies: a checklist

(1)   Have you established a regular study schedule?

(2)   If not, should you have a regular study schedule?

(3)   Where is the best place for you to work?

(4)   Do you waste time finding the bits and pieces before you start working?

(5)   Is your desk or table cluttered?

(6)   Are you doing enough reading?

(7)   When is the best time to work?

(8)   How long do you need to spend to do some useful work?

(9)   What do you do with odd bits of time, such as train journeys?

(10)   Do you sit watching television, with a guilty conscience?

(11)   Do you worry about how much work other people are doing?

(12)   Do you check that you are really working as you study?

(13)   Are you doing sufficient work?

(14)   How can you tell whether you're doing sufficient work?

An agenda which we've found useful in study-skills sessions. It can be used point-by-point as an overhead transparency or issued as a handout checklist for learners to complete prior to discussing each issue in turn.

Part 2

Starting Off, and Working Together

In this section, we look at ways of getting to know your learners and ways of helping them to work together effectively in small groups. We also present some ideas about ways of helping learners make the best use of other people, including yourself.

9

Helping learners tell you what they already know

It has been said that for more than half the time that learners spend in formal teaching/learning situations, they are listening to things they already know. The following suggestions can help overcome such a situation.

1   Help learners to value **what they already know**. Suggest to them that among their greatest resources is their existing knowledge.

2   **Give learners a list of questions** and ask them to privately brainstorm which questions they can already answer. This can be used to boost their confidence and to formulate the agenda for further work.

3   **Try a 'public' brainstorm** on what your learners already know. Display round the room sets of questions on flipcharts, and ask learners to go round putting ticks beside the questions they can definitely answer, crosses beside those they can't answer, and question marks beside those they think they may be able to answer.

4   **Conduct a group brainstorm**. Ask learners in groups to list things they already know about particular topics, then allow members of different groups to explain particular things in more detail to other groups.

5   Allocate different topics to different groups. Ask each group to prepare **a mind-map of things they already know** about their topic on a flipchart. Ask groups to exhibit their flipcharts, and stand by them explaining their mind-maps to learners from other groups touring the exhibition.

6   In groups, ask learners to **explain things to each other**. Ask each learner to choose something he or she already knows, then explain it to the rest of the group. Probably the greatest benefit comes with finding the words to explain things, thereby consolidating understanding.

7 Ask learners in groups to identify **questions that they are able to answer**. Let volunteers from each group explain the answers to chosen questions to the whole class.

8 **Devise pre-tests**, which are to be used to find out what learners already know, but not to 'test' them in a threatening way. Explain that the objective is to show them how much they already know, and to let you see what you don't need to explain to them.

9 Provide a selection of typical formal assignment questions (or typical examination questions) early in the study programme, and ask groups of learners to prepare *outline* **answers to questions of their choice** (taking far less time than writing out full answers). Discuss with the whole class the strengths of each outline answer, and point out any important things that would need to be added to the outlines to lead to good full answers.

10 Give out Post-it slips to the whole class. Ask everyone to write out **questions they already know the answers to**, and add their names to the Post-its before displaying them on a wall. Use the collected Post-its as the start of an agenda, addressing both the knowledge learners already have and the gaps you identify in the total pattern of knowledge.

10

Sharing the syllabus

Almost certainly one of the first things you were given when you began to prepare to teach your first course was syllabus documentation of one kind or another. Strangely, despite the fact that a syllabus is written to describe what is to be learned, such documents don't always find their way into the hands of learners themselves. Here are some suggestions about how you can use a syllabus to help structure a learning programme.

1   Check whether your learners already have **copies of syllabus documentation** (for example, in a course or departmental handbook). If they have not, give them at least a copy of your own part of their syllabus, and if possible the rest as well.

2   When learners know what they are expected to be learning, they're in a better position to go about their task of learning it. It helps them if you **translate their syllabus into learning objectives or learning outcomes**, so that they can see exactly what sort of things they are, in due course, going to be expected to achieve.

3   Learning objectives can sometimes seem rather remote and academic. In some cases, it is better to translate syllabus content into **statements of the competences** that learners will be required to demonstrate later in their studies. Competence descriptions can be made more meaningful by providing learners with examples or demonstrations of the skills and abilities they in turn will develop.

4   A syllabus (or a translation into objectives or competence statements) is good for letting learners know *what* they will be learning, but sometimes they also need some explanation regarding *why* **they are going to learn particular things**. It is not always obvious to them why they have to learn things – and naturally, if they can't see a good *reason* for learning something, they're not going to put much energy into trying to learn it.

5   A syllabus provides a useful map of a course. The map is made much more useful by adding some details regarding **the timescales involved**. For example, it may take several weeks to 'crack' an important early part of a syllabus, while some later parts may be very straightforward thereafter.

6   Clarify the 'learning map' even further by explaining to learners **which processes will be used** as they cover the various parts of their syllabus. For example, some things will be covered by lectures, others may be dealt with in seminars and tutorials, and yet other things may be delegated altogether to learners to undertake by private reading, group work, or using open-learning packages.

7   There will be occasions when it is best for you (and for your learners) **to depart from any published syllabus**. For example, when it is relevant to develop a topical theme to illustrate a fundamental principle, it may be useful to cover completely new ground with them. Let them know of such 'departures' – and particularly let them know which parts of the 'old' syllabus have now been replaced.

8   In any syllabus, it's unlikely that everything will be covered in an 'even' manner. Let learners know **which parts of the syllabus you'll be going into in depth,** and which you'll just be skimming over. Confirm with them the respective expectations regarding assessment of the 'in-depth' versus 'surface' parts.

9   Towards the end of a course, the syllabus (and its various 'translations' and explanations) should provide learners with a solid basis upon which to work out information about the balance of examinations that they will sit. Make sure that you write **examination questions with the syllabus very much in mind,** so reducing the possibility that learners find unexpected questions for which they could not reasonably have prepared.

10   Time often runs out. When this happens, **'let learners off the hook'** regarding parts of the syllabus that are not going to be covered. Resist the temptation to cram the last few lectures full of all the remaining parts of the syllabus – if exams are coming up shortly, few learners are going to spend much time on newly acquired information in any case.

11

Learning names

People in general tend to take more notice of people they know. Your learners will take more notice of you if they feel that they know you and, above all, that you know them. Getting their names right is a useful step towards building up the sort of relationship which fosters learning.

1   Think how *you* feel when **someone gets your name wrong** – especially someone you would have expected to know it. One of the problems with large groups is that members of the group can feel quite anonymous and alone. Decide to tackle the situation.

2   At the beginning of the course, ask learners **'what do you *want* to be called?'**. The names they give you will be more accurate than your printed class-lists, and you'll quickly find out whether Victoria wants to be called Vicky, Patricia – Pat, Cedric – 'Al'.

3   At early stages it's useful to give learners **sticky labels** to write their names on in bold felt-tip pen. This gives you the chance to call them by the name they prefer – and gives them the chance to start getting to know each other.

4   In a group session involving 10–20 learners, try a round as follows: **'Tell us your name, and tell us something *about* your name'**. This can be a good icebreaker, and can be very memorable too, helping people develop association-links with the names involved.

5   An alternative round is to get the learners sitting in a circle. Ask one to say his or her name, then the person to the left to say, **'I am ... and this is my friend ...'**. Carry on round the circle, adding one name at each stage, until someone goes right round the circle correctly.

6   A further alternative is to ask learners to introduce themselves, stating first their names and then **two 'likes' and two 'dislikes'**.

7   An alternative way of using a 'likes/dislikes' round can be asking the learners to find **someone else in the group with similar likes and dislikes,** and to form a duo or trio to prepare a poster or short sketch illustrating their shared feelings.

8   To help you to get to know their names, once you have a **complete list** of the names, ask people from your list at random some (easy) questions.

9   In tutorials, laboratories and other places where small groups of learners are sitting in particular places for a while, it is useful to give the learners each a **'place card'** (a folded A5 sheet of card serves well) and to write their names on both sides of the card and place the cards on the tables or benches (or at their feet if sitting without tables). Cards can be seen at a distance much better than labels. This allows you to address individuals by name, and also helps them to get to know each other's names.

10 When you know all the (preferred) names of members of a large group, make an **acetate sheet** with all the names on it, and use this to structure seminar groups or syndicate groups. Putting an asterisk beside the names of convenors (and rotating such roles as successive tasks are issued) gradually helps you get to know all the names of learners even in quite large groups. Seeing each other's names on the screen is a way of helping large groups not to feel so anonymous or 'lonely'.

12

Helping learners benefit from your tutorials

Despite the fact that relatively little real learning happens during most lectures, learners tend to regard lectures as more important than tutorials. This is compounded by many lecturers treating tutorials as relatively ad hoc occasions. The following suggestions may help tutorials deliver greater learning payoffs.

1 **Get to know the names** of the learners in your tutorial groups. They will regard the tutorial as more important if they feel that they are known to you, and that you will notice if they are not present.

2 **Avoid the temptation** to use tutorials to elaborate on things that have been covered in lectures. It is all too easy for tutorials to degenerate into an extension of lectures, and for learners to be as passive in tutorials as they are in most lectures.

3 Make it clear to learners that there are parts of their course which will be covered **only in tutorials**, and that these parts will be assessed in the same way as the lecture content of the course.

4 Whenever possible, brief learners in advance on the topics to be processed in **forthcoming tutorials**. Give them something specific to prepare for each tutorial, and spend some (but not all) of the time letting them share and discuss what they have prepared. Always have something up your sleeve for learners to do or discuss during tutorials, for those occasions when none of the learners brings questions or problems.

5 Explain to learners that tutorials are usually **the best times to ask you detailed questions** or to ask for explanations of things they don't yet understand. Suggest that they jot questions and issues down as they arise, and bring their lists to each tutorial. Spend some time during each tutorial dealing with these questions or issues.

6   Give learners suggestions to help them **integrate** the things you cover in tutorials with the rest of their experiences on the course. For example, suggest they keep a learning-log or diary to remind them of the main issues and questions which were dealt with during tutorials.

7   **Use tutorials to get feedback** on how learners are finding lectures and practical work. Check whether or not they have mastered things that have been covered already. Have additional tasks and practice exercises to hand, which you can use during tutorials, or issue to learners to try on their own later.

8   **Use tutorials to help learners work together**. Use tutorials for allowing learners to bring forward the products of tasks they have undertaken collaboratively. When a tutorial group really 'gels', learners will often continue to work informally in the same group.

9   Ask learners direct questions about **how they are finding your tutorials**. For example, by asking them to tell you what they would like you 'to stop, to start, and to continue', you can very quickly gain useful information to help you structure future tutorials.

10   Use tutorials **to draw together themes** from different parts of their course. It is often useful to invite colleagues in to contribute to specific tutorials, when the need arises to weld links between interrelated topics.

13

Helping learners benefit from seminars

Some courses have lectures, seminars and tutorials, and it's not always clear to learners how these respective teaching/learning situations are different. Probably the main features that distinguish seminars from tutorials are that each seminar is planned around a definite topic or issue, and that learners are progressively expected to prepare themselves to take the lead in seminars.

1 **Work out a seminar schedule**, and publish this along with your lecture schedule. This can help learners to see which topics or issues are going to be covered in depth in seminars.

2 As the course progresses, brief individual learners (or small groups) **to prepare for forthcoming seminars**, for example to give a 15-minute review of a topic, then open it up for discussion (with you as an expert witness only when needed).

3 **Agree ground rules for seminars**. These can include things such as punctuality, contribution, preparation and record-keeping. If, for example, learners take turns preparing a short résumé of what was covered in seminars, each member of the group gradually builds up a supplementary set of learning resource materials.

4 When a seminar is being used for an in-depth discussion of something that learners have covered in lectures (or from directed reading), facilitate the generation of a **list of questions**. This can be done by writing up learners' questions on a flipchart or markerboard (and can be done even more rapidly by issuing Post-its to everyone, and asking them to write their questions concisely and put them up for display).

5 Where possible, use seminars for appropriate parts of **assessed coursework**. The smaller groups involved in seminars can more easily participate in self-assessment and peer-assessment processes, giving learners the chance to gain a detailed perspective of the sort of assessment criteria which may be involved in later exams.

6 Where individual learners or groups are being assessed on the basis of their contributions to seminars (for example, giving presentations, tabling a paper, leading a discussion) **give them adequate time to prepare their contributions,** and clarify the way the seminars will be conducted and assessed.

7 Use seminar sessions to build **flexibility** into the overall course. For example, give learners choices from which to select the exact topics and formats of their forthcoming contributions. It can often help to invite an 'expert witness' from outside the course to contribute to particular seminars that learners themselves have requested – indeed the learners themselves can be given the task of finding such a person.

8 It can be useful to bring in (for example) third-year learners to lead a series of seminars with first-year learners. The more experienced learners can often explain things in a **more understandable** way than someone like yourself who has probably 'known them for a long time'. Additionally, explaining things to less experienced learners is one of the best ways of deepening their own understanding of the topics they're explaining.

9 Experiment with ways of trying to **keep everyone involved** in seminar sessions. For example, writing questions (or conclusions) on pieces of paper or overhead transparencies can overcome the problem of some learners talking too much while others hardly talk at all.

10 Use seminars on specific topics to **generate lists of learners' questions and problems** from which to select the most important ones to use as the basis for a forthcoming large-group lecture.

14

Helping learners participate in seminars

Many tutors and lecturers find it an uphill struggle to get learners to contribute to seminars. It seems that as long as a tutor is prepared to talk, learners will gladly listen. Below we list some suggestions for helping 'coerce' learners into a more active mode in seminars.

1   **Recognize that some learners may be quite shy**. Avoid bullying them into participation in seminars, especially near the beginning of a course when they may be feeling insecure, and when they may take even slight embarrassment too seriously.

2   Get learners talking to each other using **non-threatening situations** such as 'icebreakers'. Build up your own stock of short icebreakers, so that you can regularly start off a seminar session in an informal 'fun' way.

3   When it is intended that learners make substantial contributions to a particular seminar, **give them a helpful briefing the week before**, so that anyone who is nervous has the opportunity to do adequate preparation, and will feel more at ease about the prospect of contributing.

4   Discuss with learners the **value** they can derive from seminars, and particularly help them to see that the more they contribute to seminars, the more they will learn themselves.

5   Ensure that **learners don't fall into the trap** of thinking that because seminars are less formal than lectures, they are less important. In lectures, explain now and then that 'the important issues here will form the basis of your seminars in the next week or two'.

6   Allow learners to participate **in different ways** in seminars. For example, some will readily talk and discuss, while others will prefer to prepare a handout, or poster, or overhead transparency to constitute their contribution to the seminar.

7   Divide learners into **discussion groups** for (say) 15 minutes, then allow volunteers from each group to report back in whatever format they prefer to use (giving a suggested maximum time for each report).

8   Establish with the learners some **ground rules for contributions to seminars**. Help them to work out practical criteria which the group can adopt. When the ownership of the ground rules rests with the learners themselves, they are more likely to try to live up to the criteria, including everyone contributing.

9   **Come quickly to the rescue** if particular learners seem seriously uncomfortable as they contribute to a seminar. Get to know which ones are 'robust' enough to weather any difficulties, and which ones will appreciate your helpful intervention.

10   Consider the possibilities of having **more than one kind of seminar grouping**. For example, you could use 'home groups' as an on-going support-building process throughout the course, and differently constituted 'task groups' for particular topics or purposes. This helps avoid the problems that can occur when a particular group does not 'gel', as it is then not the only group in which each of its members works.

15

Encouraging peer-support groups

In practice, learners often find that they learn at least as much from each other as from any other source (including reference materials and tutors). However, they often feel that somehow they're not intended to cooperate actively with each other as part of their day-to-day learning strategy. The following suggestions may help them change this view.

1   **Show learners how much they learn from their peers**. Remind them that they have access to their peers for many more hours per week than they have access to 'expert witnesses' such as lecturers or tutors.

2   **Point out the value of 'informal' groups** in addressing problems that are common to most members of the group (including parts of subjects everyone is having difficulty with). By putting their heads together, the members of a group can more quickly find a way of addressing a problem.

3   Suggest that learners in peer-support groups do a **'SWOT' (strengths, weaknesses, opportunities, threats) analysis**, identifying the total strengths and weaknesses of the group, and working out what opportunities there are for the group to be a useful part of the learning processes of its members, and working out what threats the group as a whole perceives (as a first step to devising ways of countering the threats).

4   Encourage peer-support groups to make an **inventory of the resources available to them**, including tutors, learners in the next year up, counsellors and advisers, and textual or computer-based resources.

5   Point out the benefits of peer-support groups when members have **individual or personal problems**. It can be much less threatening to share such problems with some well-known colleagues than to admit them to a tutor. Often, members of the group can provide all the help and support that may be needed. Alternatively, members of the group can advise when a problem really does need some expert help.

6   Try to identify some learners (past or present) who have found peer-support groups very valuable. Ask them to provide **case-study evidence about how they used their group**, and what sorts of problems the group successfully handled. The evidence could be presented in person to a class, or as a video, or as a short written case-study.

7   Accept that **some learners will prefer to maintain their independence and privacy**, and will resent any attempt to force them to participate in informal peer-support groups. If such learners are manipulated into joining such groups, they can have a damaging effect on the group. Allow learners the choice of whether or not to engage in peer-support networks, possibly even suggesting that those who wish to maintain their independence and distance form their own like-minded group!

8   When devising coursework tasks and assignments, **offer choices**, including tasks designed to be done as group exercises as well as tasks designed for independent work.

9   Try out some **team-building exercises** in seminars and tutorials, allowing learners to see for themselves the different roles that can be played by members of an effective team. Encourage learners to put what they learn about teamwork into practice in their own ways.

10   **Build up a bank of 'learners' problems' scenarios**. Spend a little time giving groups of learners 'a problem' and asking them to work out a plan of action to overcome the problem. Give each group a different problem, to avoid the report-back stage becoming repetitive. Ask learners to contribute (anonymously if they wish) to the bank of problems for future use.

16

Helping learners learn from each other

Learners need encouragement to capitalize on the fact that they can learn a great deal from each other. The competitive culture often prevents them from deriving maximum benefit from each other, yet a group always has a greater amount of knowledge, experience and competence than its individual members.

1   **Encourage the formation of study syndicates**. If these are formed spontaneously by learners, there is the benefit of ownership of the group by the learners comprising it.

2   **Promote the benefits of being skilled in group work**. These include the development of leadership skills and responsibility for their own actions. The benefits also include the development of the ability to be led, which in the context of working with others is as important an attribute as that of leadership.

3   **Provide time for study syndicates to work**. For example, if formal classes run from 9.00–10.00, then 11.00–12.00, groups can work independently from 10.00–11.00, both on tasks arising from the earlier class, and on matters coming up in the subsequent one.

4   **Provide space suitable for study-syndicate work**. At its simplest, a table and chairs are all groups require – preferably in a room where groups can make some noise (not a typical library). Accessories such as blackboards, whiteboards or flipcharts can help the groups focus their activities.

5   **Help learners to distinguish between collaboration and cheating**. Learning from other members of the group should be regarded as productive. The only activity which should be regarded as cheating is failure to make an appropriate contribution to the work of the group.

6   **Let learners learn by assessing each other's efforts**. Help them to identify the criteria by which they can assess each other's work. Applying assessment criteria is an excellent way to learn.

7   **Encourage learners to quiz each other**. Rapid informal practice at answering questions is good practice for answering questions in more formal situations including exams. Learners answering each other's questions are less likely to be able to 'con' themselves about which questions they can answer than when working alone.

8   **Give opportunities for learners to teach each other**. The act of explaining something to someone else is one of the most powerful ways of learning. If each member of the group explains a selected topic to the rest of the group, the total learning achieved by the group is maximized.

9   **Ask groups of learners to brainstorm questions**. Knowing the right questions is often more than halfway towards being able to answer them effectively. Ask groups to prioritize their lists of questions. Where some questions require the expert assistance of the teacher, it is comforting that the questions have a degree of anonymity, belonging to the group rather than to particular individuals.

10   **Devise some tasks which are best done by groups** rather than by individuals. Break tasks into a number of complementary parts, where bringing together the parts can occur naturally in groups.

17

Helping learners use mentors

A mentor is sometimes defined as 'a trusted colleague'. An alternative way of thinking of a mentor is 'someone who has done' helping 'someone who is just starting to do'. It can be highly profitable for learners to find themselves a mentor and to make good use of such a person. Here are some suggestions.

1   Explain that (particularly with large numbers of learners) the tutor–learner relationship is necessarily **not quite as 'personal'** as can be a mentor–learner relationship. Therefore, it is useful for learners to seek some other person who can 'help to keep them going'.

2   It is worth thinking about the **conflict that sometimes arises** between tutoring, advising and assessing. This can limit the amount of help tutors can be seen to give learners. A neutral 'third party' such as a mentor is able to give help and advice even on sensitive areas such as assessment.

3   Explain to learners the **different sorts of 'mentor'** they may wish to choose from. For example, mature learners may already have a spouse or partner who is in an ideal position to fulfil the role of a mentor. Part-time learners may have supervisors or managers who can make very effective mentors. First-year learners may know someone from a more advanced stage of the course who is willing to act as a mentor for them.

4   **Get learners to work out the roles a mentor could play for them**. For example, 'someone to moan to', 'someone to go to when the going is tough', 'someone to help when decisions are to be made', 'simply someone who will listen', 'someone who's been there before and who will offer advice', 'someone who can step in and help solve problems', and so on.

5   **What's in it for the mentor?** Get learners to work out how they can make mentoring a two-way beneficial exchange. For many mentors, the satisfaction of feeling that they are giving useful help will be enough.

6   If you are in a position to arrange a 'supply' of potential mentors (for example if you can enlist some third-year learners to mentor first-year learners), it can be worthwhile to **arrange a mentor-training workshop**, helping mentors to work out the sorts of things they can help with, and also when *not* to try to help (such as with personal problems which need expert help).

7   Probably the best way to get a feel for mentoring is **to be one and to have one**. Many organizations now use mentoring systems of one kind or another for newcomers. Consider whether you could be involved in something similar in your own department or organization.

8   Alert learners to the **dangers of the 'competitive culture'** they may have come from. The education systems often tend to condition learners to try to work on their own, whereas in the world of work, employers want people who can get on well with each other. Mentoring is a useful process for developing interpersonal and social skills for both mentors and learners.

9   It can be useful for mentors and learners to work to an **on-going negotiated agreement** regarding their respective roles and responsibilities. Suggest that learners can draw up proposals for their part of such an agreement, and offer these to mentors.

10   Despite all the advantages of mentoring, **accept** that there will be some learners who simply do not wish to enter into this sort of arrangement. If they remain unconvinced of the benefits, their right to learn in their own independent way needs to be respected.

18

Being an expert witness

With increasing recognition of the value of 'learning-by-doing', the role of tutors has changed from being 'founts of knowledge' to being facilitators of learning. However, if tutors are to be as helpful to learners as possible, it is useful for them to be available as a 'learning resource' at suitable times and in suitable ways.

1   The simplest way of being an expert witness is to be available to **answer questions** that learners come up with. Since it is not normally possible to answer questions very efficiently in large-group teaching/ learning situations, it is worth using one or more of the suggestions below to 'collect and focus' the questions.

2   **'Taking written questions'** is a useful thing to do when large groups of learners are involved. For example, you can advise that at the end of the lecture, you would like slips of paper with written questions (with names, or anonymous) to be passed forward to you, and that you will deal with these at the beginning of the next large-group session.

3   When armed with a set of questions collected as above, you can expect that there will be **considerable overlaps** between questions. It's worth finding the three most common questions, and preparing a question/answer overhead transparency or handout, so that learners are able to 'capture' your answers to the main questions.

4   When named individuals supply you with **'minority'** questions, it can be worth waiting until you have the chance to answer them directly to the people concerned (for example, in a tutorial, or one-to-one interview) rather than giving the large group your answer.

5   You may alternatively wish to use **tutorials** for dealing with all questions from learners. A disadvantage of this is that not all tutorial groups may benefit from your 'expert witness' answers to the same questions.

6   It can be useful to establish some ground rules regarding the **sorts of questions you are willing to answer,** as opposed to those questions where you really intend learners to go about finding their own answers without your help.

7   When setting project work, seminar preparation and so on, you may wish to be **available to each group** in an 'expert witness' capacity. This may be restricted to particular stages of the work (for example, when an action plan for the project work has been made). Alternatively, you could arrange to be available at a particular time for consultation.

8   One important area of your 'expert witness' expertise is to do with the fact that **you yourself** have learned the subject successfully. How best to go about learning particular aspects of your subject is useful information to make available to learners.

9   When it is possible for you to work with colleagues in team-teaching processes, it is often useful for you to be an 'expert witness' for a **colleague's group of learners and vice versa**. This can help learners to benefit from the different perspectives that tutors necessarily have; this helps learners to gain a more balanced overall view.

10   The most direct ways that learners will use you as an 'expert witness' are normally in connection with **assessment of their work** – coursework and/or examinations. Many other suggestions in this book are intended to help you share your expertise with learners in the context of assessment.

Part 3

Lectures and Written Work

Next, we offer an assortment of suggestions relating to some of the main processes used in teaching and learning, ranging from lectures to written work. As is the case throughout this book, we do not intend to provide 'teaching tips' as such, rather we have tried to offer suggestions regarding how learners themselves can be led towards increased success and effectiveness in the various tasks and situations they meet.

19

Helping learners make the most of your lectures

Learners normally regard lectures as very important, yet during lectures they tend to be passive and poor 'receivers' if they are allowed to be so. The following suggestions can help learners approach your lectures more proactively.

1   **Let learners know what will be coming up in the next lecture** (or even give them a plan of a whole set of lectures). Suggest that learners (individually or in groups) brainstorm what they already know about the topic, before coming to the lecture.

2   Sometimes at the start of a lecture, allow a few minutes for learners to privately brainstorm their answers to **'what I already know about ...'**. A further way of helping learners to tune in to your lecture is to display last year's exam question on the topic of the lecture, at the beginning or end of the lecture, so that learners are alerted regarding what they may be expected to do with the content.

3   Suggest sometimes at the start of a lecture that groups of learners brainstorm **'what we want to find out today about ...'**. Use the results of such brainstorms as an agenda for your lecture, making sure that you address as many as possible of the questions learners have posed.

4   **Encourage learners to review the content of each lecture.** For example, ask them to decide what they would write down as 'the one thing I really need to remember from this lecture', or the 'three most important points mentioned today'. Suggest that they do this individually, then compare their decisions with some other learners.

5   Point out the benefits of *making* notes, rather than simply *taking* notes. Explain how easy it is to be mentally quite passive if just writing down the words they hear or see on the screen, whereas it is possible to be much more active by putting ideas and concepts into their own words as the lecture proceeds.

6   Suggest that learners allocate a few minutes two or three days later to **process each lecture systematically**, by jotting on one side of a small card the key issues covered by the lecture, and on the reverse some questions they need to become able to answer about the lecture.

7   Suggest that learners spend a few minutes **in a small group** reviewing each lecture, using the notes and questions they prepared while reviewing it individually. During this group review, learners can add each other's questions and summary points to their own collections, so that each member of the group leaves with better resources than they started with.

8   Give out Post-its to the whole group during a lecture and ask everyone to write on them **three or more questions covered by past lectures**, which they think it important to be able to answer. Stick the Post-its on a wall, and 'tour' the agenda of questions, giving your own (authoritative) comments regarding the relative importance of particular questions.

9   Now and then, use some time in lectures or tutorials to ask groups of learners to **create 'maps'** of the content of the lecture course to date.

10   **Get quick (and sharp) feedback during your course of lectures**. One way is to give out Post-its and ask learners to write the heading words 'stop', 'start' and 'continue' across the top of them, then tell you things they would like you to do under each heading. The Post-its can be anonymously stuck to a wall, and the 'stop' entries will often alert you to things you had no idea were amiss. The 'start' entries can alert you to things that you can address in the next few lectures. The 'continue' entries are the good news.

20

Overhead projection transparencies which help learners

The overhead projector is now the most common way of displaying visual information to learners, particularly in large-group situations. A major advantage of overhead projection is that you can see your audience as you speak. The following guidelines may help your learners get the most from your use of the overhead projector.

1 Make sure that each transparency will be **visible from the back of the largest room** you are likely to use, even by someone without perfect eyesight.

2 **Ensure that your transparencies will fit any projector**. Many projectors have a plate of approximately A4 size (and can usually be arranged for vertical or lateral display). Some projectors have square screens, a little less than A4 height in both directions.

3 Copying down words from transparencies is not the most productive of learning activities. Where possible, issue handout materials which **already contain the wording from your principal overhead transparencies**. This can be done either by including the wording in the text of your handouts, or by preparing an appendix of photo-reduced transparencies.

4 Consider the possibility of issuing **printed versions of your overheads as a handout in their own right**. Learners can use such handouts to add notes from the discussions and explanations on each point on the overheads.

5 The medium is the message? If your overhead transparencies look **professional and 'credible'**, learners will trust your message much more than if you are using rough, hand-drawn transparencies. Desktop publishing systems can be used to prepare high-quality transparencies very quickly.

6   **Don't remove transparencies too quickly**. Learners have very different speeds of noting down points from transparencies. They feel cheated if the images are removed before they've finished with them. Learners need more time than it would take for them to simply *read* the transparencies.

7   **Add things to your transparencies during discussions**. If the transparencies are prepared with permanent pens (or photocopied from a desktop publishing system printout), you can use soluble ink to add things coming up in discussion, and then remove them ready for your next use of the transparency.

8   **Don't over-use 'progressive reveal' techniques** (showing transparencies a bit at a time by gradually moving a masking sheet of paper). Some learners feel manipulated if they are continually 'controlled' in this way. And if you do reveal progressively, make sure that you keep up with yourself!

9   **Use colour**. With desktop-produced transparencies, use coloured acetate sheets to add variety. With hand-made transparencies, use a variety of ink colours (but don't use orange or yellow, which don't show up at all well, and remember that red doesn't show up well at the back of a large room).

10   At conferences (and in other people's lectures), **note the styles** of overhead transparencies which are well received by audiences, and experiment with things which seem to work effectively for other people.

21

Handling other people's bad teaching

It would be a strange world if every teacher were 'perfect', and all lectures, tutorials, seminars and laboratory classes were deep and enjoyable learning experiences. Assuming you've done your best to serve your own learners as well as you can, you may still need to help them overcome the shortcomings of colleagues of yours. Obviously this is a sensitive situation, but we hope the following suggestions may help.

1   **Encourage learners to form self-help groups** and (among other things) to use these to compensate for bad teaching. When several learners put their heads together, they can often find ways of developing their understanding of the subjects concerned.

2   **Where possible, take part in team-teaching situations**. For example, sit in on colleagues' lectures and then run tutorials with their learners (and vice versa). You may be surprised how useful it can be to witness other people's ways of teaching – learning both things to emulate and things to avoid. Team-teaching situations are one of the least threatening ways for you to demonstrate good practice which some of your colleagues may need to develop themselves.

3   **Spread the load**. Help to structure the teaching in your department so that learners experience a variety of teaching styles. This is preferable to the possibility of some groups of learners being overdosed with any one style (especially a difficult one).

4   **Help learners take more responsibility for their own learning,** by building in appropriate study-skills sessions or giving out study-skills aids. The more learners can gain control over the ways they learn, the less susceptible to 'bad teaching' they become.

5   Seek feedback from your own learners, **and show colleagues how useful the feedback can be** in developing your own teaching style. Be ready to tell colleagues about changes you made in your own approaches based on feedback from learners.

6   When learners have unsatisfactory learning of material that is a prerequisite to your own work with them, it may save you much time and energy in the long run to prepare an **introductory learning package** to help them reach the starting point you wish them to accomplish before your own work with them. Such a package could be used instead of one or two of your timetabled sessions with them, so that they could catch up at their own pace and in their own ways (preferably working in informal groups where possible).

7   Where bad teaching has led to unproductive learning habits, take time with your learners to **alert them to the dangers** they may be in. Help them identify 'hang-ups' they have been left with because of their unsatisfactory experiences.

8   **Try to avoid jealousies and mistrust**. Don't be tempted to criticize colleagues when working with learners. Concentrate on ways the learners can be helped to compensate for whatever is missing in those parts of the teaching that are lacking in quality.

9   **Take part in departmental seminars about teaching and learning**. Give examples of things that have gone well in your own teaching – and (even better) things that did not go well at first, and what you did to improve the situation. Take care that the finger of blame is not pointed at whoever most needs to take note of your contributions to such seminars.

10   **Share teaching/learning resources you have made**. Contributing to a bank of overhead transparencies, or a collection of handouts, or a set of assignment questions, can be a useful way of spreading good practice.

22

Helping learners make notes

Learners spend a significant amount of time writing notes. However, often they are 'taking' notes (a passive process) rather than 'making' notes (a more active process). The following ideas may help your learners make more useful notes.

1   Remind learners how passive it is **just to copy down the words** they hear in lectures, or the words they see on a screen, or the words they see in a book. It is quite possible to copy page after page in such a way, without ever really thinking about what the words actually mean.

2   Suggest that in all forms of note-making, learners try to put things **into their own words**. This automatically engages their brains in working out what the words may mean.

3   Many learners seem to have been taught to be economical with paper! They feel that they have to fill each page up uniformly, starting at the top left hand corner, and working down to the bottom right hand corner. Remind learners that if each page of their notes looks similar, they will be missing out on the **strong 'visual' side of their thinking**. Making patterned notes, for example, is a way of using both verbal and visual memory and interpretation.

4   **Advise against uniformity**. If (as in most books, including this one) everything is in the same size of print (or handwriting), it is hard to tell the 'meat' from the 'bones'. Suggest that learners capture the shades of importance of different ideas, and translate them into something visual in their notes – different colours, different sizes of writing, boxes and so on.

5   Suggest that learners write down *their* **questions and** *their* **comments**, and interweave these with notes they make. For example, in lectures, many learners *think* of questions they would like to find the answers to, but after an hour or two the questions have evaporated from their memories. When the questions are actually written into learners' notes, they then have the opportunity to go about seeking the answers.

6   Suggest that learners **'do something with' their notes**, regularly, rather than just pile them up on a shelf. Making summaries, making additions, adding new topics, deciding what the most important points are, are all ways of turning a set of notes into an active learning resource, rather than a dead collection of information.

7   Encourage learners to work together in small groups, informally, **improving their notes** by adding things that each has thought of. A small syndicate can make a much more useful set of notes than an individual.

8   **Remind learners that it's not enough just to have 'captured the words'.** For example, if a handout is given out in a lecture, learners often switch off, because they believe that they already 'have' the lecture. They would be much better advised to edit the handout and make additions to it throughout the lecture.

9   Advise learners of the benefits of **continually 'distilling'** the information they collect, for example onto small summary cards. This can help them to whittle down large amounts of miscellaneous information to manageable proportions, helping them make easier work of revision for exams.

10   **Remind learners to take care of their notes** – and not to 'put them all into one basket'. There are many horror stories around of learners whose one set of notes was lost or destroyed at a crucial stage just before the exams.

23

Helping learners develop essay-writing skills

Despite the fact that essay writing counts significantly in the assessment of learners (both in exams and continuous assessment schemes), learners are often left to pick up the necessary skills by trial and error. They can be helped to deliver better essays by spending a little time working out where the 'goalposts' are.

1   **Explain the benefits of becoming good at writing essays**. The obvious benefits relate to assessment – in many programmes of study, assessment is predominantly on the basis of essays (whether written in examination rooms, or as coursework).

2   **Encourage learners to make essay plans rather than starting 'cold'**. Making a plan can save a lot of time in the long run. When a plan has been made, it is possible to reflect on the plan for a while, improving the order and coherence of the essay in due course. Remind learners that structure is often as important as content.

3   **Bring to learners' attention the importance of a good introduction**. The first paragraph or two can set the reader's expectations. This in turn can have a marked bearing on the grade or score which the essay earns.

4   **Remind learners that a paragraph should essentially be something containing a single idea**. Breaking the essay into 'good' paragraphs helps set out the unfolding ideas, and makes it much easier for the reader to follow arguments and discussions. Many people (including many assessors) skim read, by reading the first (and maybe last) sentence of each paragraph; it is useful for learners to bear this in mind.

5   **Stress the importance of a good conclusion**. In assessed essays, this is likely to be the last part to be read before assessors decide on a grade or score. Therefore, the better the quality of the finish, the higher may be the score. Remind learners how important it is, therefore, that the conclusions focus firmly on the question or task as it was set.

6   **Help learners understand the sort of criteria which are used in assessing essays** in their particular subjects. Give them some essay titles, then share with them the sort of criteria you would be looking for in good essays.

7   **Let learners try their hands at assessing essays themselves**. Give them some specimen essays and ask them to analyse them in terms of virtues and faults. This works best when learners can subsequently work in small groups, comparing their lists of virtues and faults and generating a prioritized list of both.

8   **Facilitate learners generating assessment criteria for essays**. This can be done using specimen essays or using essay titles. Ask learners to work out individually (say) 'six important things that should be in an essay on . . .', and then discuss their criteria with others.

9   It is possible to make several essay plans in the time that it takes to create one fully fledged essay. The thinking and learning that occurs in making several essay plans is, however, much greater than that in simply creating one finished essay. It is therefore useful to facilitate a session where learners **generate a series of essay plans**, then 'mark' the plans using criteria they devise themselves.

10   Advise learners to prepare coursework essays in good time, so that they can **'put them out of sight' for a few days** then come back to them 'with fresh eyes'. With creative writing, subconscious thought processes go on continuously, and the benefits are lost if there is no opportunity to capture 'second thoughts' and 'considered views' and add them to the essays.

24

Helping learners develop report-writing skills

The nature and style of report-writing varies considerably from one discipline to another. Also, the expectations vary from one tutor to another. There are, however, some general ways that tutors can help learners avoid some of the common dangers associated with report-writing.

1   **Advise learners to start writing reports early rather than later**. For example, after completing some practical work, it is much easier to write the report when the work is fresh in their memories.

2   Point out to learners the **dangers of accumulating a backlog** of report-writing. If they have several reports awaiting completion, it is not unusual for the details of the separate pieces of work to begin to merge.

3   One of the most serious dangers of leaving report-writing till later is that learners often find themselves catching up with their report-writing while **more diligent colleagues have moved on** to revision for forthcoming exams.

4   Where learners are going to be doing a lot of report-writing, it is worth encouraging them to acquire skills at using a **desktop publishing or word-processing package**. Using such tools may be slow at first, but continued practice leads to the ability to produce professional-looking work and, more importantly, makes it much easier to edit and adjust the work as it nears completion.

5   Remind learners to pay particular attention to choosing a **suitable title** for each report. Titles become clumsy if they are too long; a short title with additional explanation as a sub-title can be more effective than a long one.

6   Remind learners to make the **aims** of each piece of work clear and concise, near the beginning of the report.

7   Most types of report contain a **summary or abstract** near the beginning. Remind learners how important this part is and suggest that they write it last, when they already know exactly what the conclusions of the work are, and how the report has been structured. This helps to guarantee that the report will 'live up to the promise of its beginning'.

8   **Discuss with learners when to use appendices**. For example, detailed descriptions of experimental procedure, or tables of data, and other illustrative material is sometimes best presented as appendices, so as not to interrupt the main flow of the discussion in a report.

9   Explain the importance of **discussion and interpretation** of data, measurements and observations. Encourage learners to give alternative hypotheses when interpretation is inconclusive, and to suggest ways that the investigation could be improved if further work is to be undertaken.

10   Even when the main findings of a report have been summarized in an abstract or summary at the start of the report, it is worth advising learners to present the main conclusions **at the end as well**. These should reflect the aims of the investigation stated at the outset of the report.

25

Helping learners learn in laboratories

In many practical subjects, learners spend a considerable proportion of their time in laboratories of one kind or another. Laboratory work is essentially hands-on, 'learning-by-doing' work. However, learners can benefit from some help in ensuring that they get the most from this kind of learning. Here are some ways you can help them.

1   Do everything you can to avoid wasted time **at the start** of laboratory sessions. Ensure that technical staff know exactly what will be required well in advance, and that they have the opportunity to have it all set up in time.

2   Avoid learners **having to 'tune in'** at the start of sessions – for example, having to read a detailed set of instructions before beginning to use some equipment. It is useful to issue such instructions (say) a week in advance, so that learners can start their practical work as soon as the session commences.

3   Learners often don't seem to know why they are doing practical work. Make **the links between theory and practical work** as clear as possible. Formulate objectives for each piece of practical work, so that learners know exactly why they're doing it.

4   Where it is necessary for learners to write down instrument readings and other quantitative data (and observations), it can be useful to develop a **structured worksheet**, so that learners have a clear frame of reference in which to carry out their work. Providing such structured 'skeletons' can be good training for later practical work, when learners need to take full responsibility for organizing their data-recording themselves.

5   Try to avoid the situation where learners undertake practical work as if they were merely 'following recipes'. Asking them to **interpret** what they observe can help to keep their attention on the meaning of what they see and measure.

6   With large practical classes, **try to avoid queuing situations**, where several learners are waiting for the availability of a particular piece of equipment. It can be useful to have several different pieces of practical work going on at once, rather than all of the group trying to do the same thing.

7   When you identify a 'log-jam' (such as something you keep having to demonstrate to learners), consider ways of preparing a **learning resource** which can do this for you. A simple clear set of step-by-step instructions may be all that is needed, or perhaps it's worth making a video so that your demonstration is available to anyone at any time.

8   One of the most significant dangers of practical work is that learners can accumulate a **backlog in their report-writing**. This can lead them to be catching up on reports when they should have been preparing for exams, and often leads to exam failures. Instituting a fairly strict regime regarding report submission will be useful to your learners, especially if you explain exactly why. Remind learners that the sooner they write a report, the less time it actually takes, as they remember better what they actually did!

9   **Make it clear to your learners how much the laboratory work contributes to their overall assessment**. This allows them to judge how much time and energy they should be spending on such work.

10   Encourage learners to try to **make sense** of what they observe and measure. When devising assessment criteria for laboratory work, make sure that important skills such as interpretation, imagination and initiative are catered for in the assessment profile.

26

Helping learners plan their projects

In many courses (and particularly in the final year of courses) learners undertake project work which counts for a significant proportion of their assessment profile. This work may take a substantial amount of their time. Spending a little time helping learners plan the way they will handle large tasks such as projects, can help them deliver much better results.

1   Encourage learners to take some time working out the **overall aim of their project**. This should answer the question 'why?'.

2   Suggest to learners that they should break down the overall aim into a **series of steps** through which the aim can be achieved. Each of these steps can then be phrased as an 'objective', helping to create a definite and tangible frame of reference around which to plan work on the project.

3   Suggest that learners look at each of the objectives they've worked out, asking **'how best can this one be achieved?'** This enables them to map out the range of processes they will need to use as they carry out the research, field work or practical work involved.

4   Having worked out an overall aim, a series of objectives and a summary of the processes to be used to achieve the objectives, it's worth turning these into **a draft outline of the proposed project**, so that feedback can be sought at this early stage. A one-page outline can be the basis for valuable feedback (from tutors, fellow learners, supervisors and so on).

5   Where projects are going to be developed by learners in groups, advise them to plan out at this stage the **respective contributions individuals are going to make to the overall product**. It can be useful for the groups to do an informal 'strengths, weaknesses, opportunities, threats' (SWOT) analysis, so that each of them contributes in the most productive manner.

6   **Advise learners to turn the project proposals into an action plan,** by adding timescales and stage deadlines. In many circumstances, it is useful to advise them to set a completion deadline using only half of the available time. This allows time for reflection and development and for the production of a better final project.

7   Where learners are developing projects in groups, it is useful to get them to add to the emerging action plan precise details of **'what is going to be done by whom, starting when and finishing when?'** This can be turned into a visual form by making a chart, with time running horizontally, tasks vertically and drawing 'bars' across the chart showing the duration of each task and writing on the bars the name of the learner who will be working on that task.

8   Before starting work on the respective tasks, it is useful for learners to start thinking about the **format** they will use to report their findings. Formats may be written reports, oral presentations, or a combination of both. Reports may be in a highly specified form, or there may be a great deal of freedom. Suggest that learners work out exactly how the results of each of the tasks in their action plans will contribute to the final reporting process.

9   A highly productive way of assisting learners to deliver projects of good quality is to help them start thinking about what the **assessment criteria** are likely to be. Often it is possible to ask the learners themselves to present a suggested framework of assessment criteria. They can then receive feedback regarding the appropriateness of the criteria they have worked out. When learners undertake project work against a clear background of the assessment criteria, their chances of achieving the criteria are maximized.

10   Lecturers, tutors (and other people) can be very useful **'expert witnesses'** during the on-going work of a project. Encourage learners to work out who they can use in such a capacity and how best to go about it.

27

Getting feedback from your learners

Feedback is an important stage in the processes by which we learn. In particular, we need feedback to develop positive feelings about what we do (and of course to find out about things we may not yet be doing well enough). The following are just some ways you can gather feedback from your learners – and thereby help to adjust your approach to help them learn more successfully.

1   **Watch their faces.** There's a wealth of information to be gained from the body language of learners in large groups, in small groups and individually. Facial expressions will often tell you things that they would not put into words.

2   **Watch their backs!** You may not be able to do this yourself, but a colleague can help you here. In a large group, it's useful to have someone 'watching from behind' now and then. You may be able to learn of things going on that you had no idea about. (Sitting at the back of the room in a brilliant lecture, I observed one learner knit solidly for the hour.)

3   **'Are there any parts you'd like me to say a bit more about?'**, is a useful question. It's better than 'Are there parts you don't understand?', or 'Any questions?' Finding out which parts 'didn't get across first time' is useful feedback in its own right. Sometimes it's easier to get such feedback in one-to-one chats or in tutorials than in a large group.

4   **Now and then give out a short questionnaire.** For example, provide your learners with some alternative 'feelings-words' to ring or underline. Possibilities include: 'bored', 'interested', 'enthused', 'puzzled', 'stimulated', 'irritated', 'tired', 'swamped', 'intimidated', 'lulled-to-sleep', 'condescended-to' and so on. Don't take offence at the negative words ringed; regard all feedback as potentially useful information. We've given an example below of a Post-it slip which we've given to learners and from which we learned useful things.

How's the course going for you?
Circle the words that apply, and add your own comments

fine	*all right*	*great*
stimulating	*too quickly*	*too slowly*
boringly	*useful*	*challenging*
know most already		*not addressing my problem*

Other comments:

---

5   When your learners have covered several topics, give them a list of what they've done, with three columns for them to tick regarding **how well they believe they understand each topic**. Column headings such as 'completely understand', 'think I understand' and 'don't yet understand' are useful. This sort of feedback gives you useful information about 'what got across and what didn't'.

6   **Occasionally give out open-ended free-response questionnaires.** For example, ask learners to write down answers (anonymously) to 'the two things I most like about the course are: . . . and the two things I like least about the course are . . .'. It's possible to get some quite hurtful replies to the latter – but all feedback is useful if you accept it in the right spirit.

7   Another way of getting mid-course feedback is to issue learners with Post-it slips and ask them to write three headings: **'stop', 'start'** and **'continue'**. Ask them then to write below each heading what they would like stop, start and continue doing in the next part of the course.

Stop	*Start*	*Continue*

8   **It's sometimes advantageous to seek feedback from groups rather than from individuals.** Asking a group to give opinions gives learners the chance to compare their views, and spares individuals being associated with particularly strong views – it's more anonymous coming from a group than from an individual. Getting a group to fill in a questionnaire can be a useful and interesting experience. Where there is disagreement on how members of the group feel about a particular question, they will often elaborate on the questionnaire (eg, three of us liked this, two of us didn't). The things that cause mixed feelings may be an important area of feedback for you.

9   **Seek feedback from individuals you happen to have occasion to talk to.** In a large group, you may only have detailed discussions with a learner now and again, but you can still get useful feedback information. 'Which bit are you finding best and why?' may sometimes be a better question than just, 'How's it going then?'

10 **Your own colleagues can give you useful feedback** – especially in team-teaching situations. The main reason why professional people don't give each other enough feedback is because they don't ask each other directly for it. You can break this chain. Many of your colleagues will have a fairly good idea about how *your* teaching is going – they pick up signals from learners all the time. These colleagues may be reluctant to volunteer the feedback to you, but when asked, they will usually tell – at least the 'good news'.

Part 4

Learning Resources

Our suggestions here are connected both with learning resources you may design for your learners, and other facilities which may be available for them to use – not least, the library.

28

Writing open-learning materials

Increasing use is being made of open and flexible learning, not only in distance-learning programmes but also as part of the processes used by learners on college-based courses. The following guidelines may help you design open-learning materials for your own learners.

1   **Map out objectives for your learners**. Choose the wording so as to help them to 'want' to achieve the objectives. Make it easy for *them* to tell when they have achieved each objective.

2   **Most learning is done by *doing***. Compose structured self-assessment questions and activities based on each of the learning objectives. Pay particular attention to the wording of these questions and activities, so that learners working alone will interpret them as intended.

3   **A vital part of learning is *feedback***. For each self-assessment question design a feedback response which does more than simply provide learners with the answer to the question. Learners need to find out the answers to their questions: *'Was I right?'* and *'If not, why not?'*

4   For each activity (usually something more open-ended or longer than a self-assessment question), **design a feedback discussion**. In these, you may not always be able to respond to *'Was I right?'* and *'If not, why not?'*, but as far as you can, respond to what learners are likely to have done with the activity.

5   Where it is not possible to set structured self-assessment questions or activities to allow learners to practise things related to particular objectives, **design tasks of a more open-ended nature**. Turn these into questions for tutor-marked assignments, where human judgement and feedback can accommodate each learner's way of trying such tasks.

6   Remembering that most open-learning tutors are not the authors of the respective materials, **design model answers and commentaries** for each tutor-marked assignment question. This allows other tutors to know how you expected the questions to be interpreted, and promotes fair and uniform assessment.

7   **Prepare 'bridges' of text and illustrations**, linking the response to one self-assessment question to the task posed by the next. Writing the content as a series of small 'bridges' ensures that you aren't tempted to create a textbook. It also ensures that any learners who simply try to read through the 'text', without trying the activities or using the feedback responses, are quickly reminded that this is not how they can learn best from open-learning materials.

8   **Try out 'chunks' of your draft open-learning materials with 'live' learners**. Observe their progress with the self-assessment questions and activities. Ask them whether they made any mistakes which weren't responded to by the feedback responses. Ask them whether there were any places where the materials were going too fast (or too slow) for them.

9   **Prepare a 'pilot version' of the complete module**, and design a short feedback questionnaire to go with it. Try out the pilot version on a sample of learners and also on a few colleagues. Collect as much feedback as you can, both from the questionnaires and from interviews (face-to-face or telephone).

10   Use the information gained from the first run of the tutor-marked assignments as a measure of how well the materials are working. **Make adjustments** (both to the materials and to the wording of the assignments) whenever common difficulties are shown by learners' attempts at the assignments.

29

Helping learners use open-learning materials

For many learners, open learning can appear to be something new. A little help regarding how best to go about handling open-learning materials can help learners maximize the benefits to them of being able to work at their own pace, at times of their own choosing, and in their own styles.

1   **Help your learners to realize how open learning works** – particularly the freedom to learn at their own pace, in places of their own choosing, and at times that suit them.

2   Remind your learners **that there's nothing new** about open or flexible learning. All learning tends to be done at people's own pace, place and times – even in the context of tutor-led programmes.

3   **Point out to your learners the value to them of learning objectives.** Show them how to use objectives as a means of mapping their progress and as a way of testing their achievement.

4   Remind your learners that most learning is 'by doing'. Point out that the activities, tasks and self-assessment questions in open-learning materials are the **'doing' opportunities**, and that if they are skipped, not much real learning can happen.

5   Explain to your learners the importance of their receiving feedback as they learn. Point out that in open-learning materials, much of this feedback tends to come from **'responses'** to activities and self-assessment questions. Remind them that such feedback will be of real value to them only *after* they've had a try at the questions and activities (in other words, looking too early at the answers will rob them of valuable learning opportunities).

6   **Guide your learners regarding what's really important and what's simply background.** Help them establish what they 'need to know' versus what is merely 'nice to know'. A quick way of doing this is to star-rate the objectives in the open-learning materials.

7 **Check that the illustrations in the open-learning materials are self-explanatory** (diagrams, graphs, tables, charts and so on). The biggest problem with many such illustrations is the uncertainty learners feel regarding 'what am I expected to do with this?' (For example, in a table of data, have they to learn it, or interpret it, or spot the trend, or something else?) A few words of guidance regarding each illustration can prevent learners wasting energy on things they need not learn.

8 **Make sure that there are sufficient opportunities for revision and consolidation.** A problem with open-learning materials is that they may cover something well, once – but then assume it's been mastered by learners. Add on revision exercises or tutor-marked assignments to help learners retain important skills and knowledge.

9 **Point out the advantages of *not* working alone when using open-learning materials.** Encourage learners to take advantage of any opportunities they get to work with a few colleagues. Show them how quickly they can break down assumptions they may have made. Remind them how useful it is to explain something to someone else.

10 **Prepare your own study guide to the open-learning materials** (even if you wrote the materials themselves). A study guide can be updated much more quickly than original materials, and can respond quickly to the problems you will be alerted to through feedback from your learners. Also, ensure that there are effective safety mechanisms for open learners who 'go off the rails' or fall too far behind. Make sure they know where to go for help, who can help them, and when is the best time to seek help.

30

Using videos to help learning

Years ago, when a television screen in a classroom was a novelty, it was more 'memorable' than it tends to be today. With television sets everywhere, attitudes to them have changed, and we don't tend to take much notice of most of what we see on the small screen. For educational television to work, therefore, it is necessary to look carefully at the intended learning outcomes.

1 **Decide exactly why you're going to use video**. It is perfectly acceptable to use it 'as a break' or 'as icing on the cake' or 'for entertainment' *as long as your learners know* your purpose.

2 When you are using video as part of your learning resources for a group of learners, **work out exactly what you intend them to be able to do after seeing the video**, that they may not have been able to do already. It's useful to give learners these 'intended learning outcomes' in advance, so they know what to take particular notice of (even subconsciously) as they view the video.

3 **Remember that concentration spans are short**, and that learners sitting quite still looking at a television screen are likely to go to sleep! A few well-chosen 'clips' may be better than a 30-minute documentary or debate – however interesting it is.

4 **When possible, get learners to create an 'agenda' before watching a video**. If they have previously thought of questions they want answered, or examples they wish to see, when they view the video they are receiving information they are looking for, rather than simply being bombarded with information.

5 **Analyse your reasons for wishing to use video**. For example, video is particularly useful not only for showing 'things in motion' but also facial expression, body-language, interpersonal behaviour and so on. Video can also give learners an impression of things they would not otherwise be able to see, such as industrial processes, distant geological features, time-lapse sequences, microscopic details and so on. Share your reasons for choosing to use video with your learners.

6   Since most people are conditioned to forget quickly what they have seen on television screens, **find ways of 'capturing' the important things**. For example, pause now and then to pose a question or two to the group of learners, or to get them discussing the implications of something they have just seen.

7   Where important conclusions are to be drawn from viewing a video, **find ways that the conclusions can be transferred to paper**. A short supporting handout can be enough to remind learners of things they were shown on the screen. Alternatively, give learners a few minutes now and then to jot down their own conclusions or reactions to what they have just seen.

8   Where learning outcomes derived from video materials are important enough to have assessment criteria directly associated with them, **make sure that learners are aware of the situation**. For example, if exam questions will require learners to use information they have gathered from videos, it is important that learners are alerted to this in advance, so that their viewing will be sufficiently active.

9   Work out whether it is best to use video with **large groups** of learners (for example, projected onto the large screen in a lecture theatre, providing a 'shared experience' for the whole group) or with **smaller tutorial groups** (where detailed discussion is more easily possible).

10   Where possible, arrange that a copy of each video can be **viewed again** by learners (for example those who may have missed the original screening, or who want to look again in more depth). It is usually possible to lodge copies of such materials in the reference section of a library or learning resources centre. Make sure that any printed briefing-sheets or handouts are also available to accompany the video there.

31

Using camcorders to make videos for your learners

We're assuming here that you have already worked out exactly why you wish to make a video for your learners and exactly why you have decided to do it yourself. These suggestions are not meant for experienced users of modern recording and editing equipment, but may be helpful if you are venturing out on your first mission with a camcorder!

1   **Don't be afraid of the machine**. You're not going to break it by pressing the wrong button at the wrong time. The worst you can do (unless you drop the machine from a reasonable height) is to make a poor recording.

2   Video tapes are cheap, and can be used over and over again anyway. In other words, **it costs nothing to practise**. As with many other skills, producing good videos is learnt better by trial and error than by reading learned treatises on cameramanship.

3   Don't film for three days and only then start to look at what you're recording. **Arrange to see the results of your recording as soon as you possibly can,** so that you can learn immediately from your mistakes – and your successes. It's useful to have a cable connector which allows your camera to be linked directly to the aerial socket of any television set, so you don't need to wait until you get to a set which can be tuned in to your camera's output.

4   **Video cameras aren't just for fast-moving objects**. Indoors or out-doors, enough is moving without your seeking out motion. Faces, leaves, traffic, etc will bring enough 'lifelikeness' to your recordings.

5   **Using a simple tripod can make a great deal of difference to your recordings**, especially if you need to use zoom facilities. Remember that at high magnification, even the slightest 'camera-shake' will seem like an earthquake on the screen.

6   **Try not to use the zoom except when really necessary.** It's very tempting to get carried away by the zoom facility, but the higher the zoom, the more you need your steadiness and expertise. Also, if you're having to use high zoom, the chances are that you're not going to be getting a good sound recording of what you're filming.

7   **When possible, take close-up shots.** These can add impact to a recording, and you may well be surprised at how well details come out in close-up (and of course, any associated sound is likely to be captured with a minimum of stray noises).

8   When you particularly wish to capture sounds, where possible use a **suitable separate microphone** rather than the one built into the camcorder. Internal microphones always suffer from at least some vibration and machine noises; a well-placed separate microphone can give much better results. Practise microphone positioning as well as practising camerawork, and learn from your successes and failures.

9   **When using a camcorder, try to avoid rapid temperature changes.** If you move a cold camera into a warm, moist environment, you are likely to risk condensation forming on the cold metal parts of the camera – not least the recording mechanisms. This can cause the tape to stick, or cause deposits to be left from the tape on the intricate innards of the camera. Water is an obvious enemy of camcorders, but remember that sand can be just as dangerous if it gets into the works.

10   **When you're ready, show your results to experienced camcorderists!** Don't defend your results – regard every criticism as useful feedback. The more criticism you can get, the faster you will build up a useful collection of techniques and wrinkles.

32

Helping learners use computer conferencing

Computer conferencing and electronic mail are widely available to learners in most large educational institutions. However, use of these media, while being readily taken up by engineering and computing learners, tends to be resisted by many other learners. The following suggestions may help you persuade your learners to benefit from using electronic mail and computer conferencing.

1   **Prepare an easy-to-read, informal guide to the basics of getting started on computer conferencing**. Assume absolutely no prior knowledge, and start with instructions about how to switch on. Give copies to everyone. Provide an introductory conference, with 'tutorial' pages which help learners to master the principal processes of adding entries and editing their entries. Make sure that the introductory conference is really easy to use (test it out on non-computer-literate colleagues first).

2   **Emphasize that learners won't blow up the mainframe!** The worst that any learners can do is to lose some of their own entries to conferences.

3   Give learners **definite, useful things** to do using computer conferencing.

4   **Set up study syndicates**, and ask each syndicate to make entries in computer conferences. This helps the computer-literate learners to teach the others how to use the system.

5   **Set up class conferences** ('private' conferences with entry restricted to particular groups of learners). Put into the conference some valuable source material of your own (for example, important lecture materials) so that learners can access it only by using the class conference.

6 **Set some assessed coursework** to be entered by learners into a computer conference. This allows all learners to see each others' work, and also to see your feedback comments to each. (Allow for the fact that the standard of the work will progressively improve as learners learn from each other and from you – the computer will record the times and dates of each entry, so you can accommodate the developing standard in the way you award credit for entries.)

7 Suggest that learners **set up their own conferences** on topics that interest them. Conference themes which can prove popular include 'music', 'sci-fi', 'the good pubs guide', 'sport', 'software', 'good second-hand clothes shops', 'hairdressers' and so on. Even when learners make frivolous entries, remember that they are still developing both communication skills and keyboard skills.

8 **Use computer conferencing as an 'agony column' for your course**. Encourage learners to enter their problems and to reply to each other's problems. Reply to important issues yourself, as 'expert witness' when appropriate.

9 **Agree on some ground rules for computer conferencing entries**. For example, language should not be obscene, entries should not 'put anyone down', sexism and racism should be strictly avoided and so on. These rules may need to be enforced strictly – if people step seriously out of line, the simplest way is to cancel their user-names.

10 **Try to extend the availability of terminals**. Some institutions have managed to create seven-days a week, 24-hours availability. Terminals can be located both in departments and in communal areas such as libraries or Students' Union premises. Make sure your learners know where all the terminals they can use are located.

33

Helping learners use the library

When they first go to a new institution, learners normally have some sort of library tour, or even some library training. However, like anything else, if it's not quickly followed up by being put into practice, much of it is forgotten.

1   Help learners to see how useful it will be to them in the long run to become **efficient at tracking down resources** in the library or learning resources centre. This will save them from wasting a considerable amount of time – often at stages in their studies when time is particularly precious.

2   **Set tasks** (for example preparations for tutorials) which require learners to track down particular reference materials. Plan the tasks so that they become experienced at using the search facilities (for example computerized catalogues) for both textbooks and journals, and then physically locating the materials.

3   Help learners to develop their abilities to **focus** on relevant source materials. Give them guidelines regarding what to look for in their particular disciplines (for example, names of writers who are particularly appropriate).

4   **Devising a piece of assessed coursework** which necessarily develops learners' information-tracking skills can be a useful way of giving them the necessary practice. One way of doing this is to ask each learner to produce an annotated bibliography of exactly 30 key references on a given topic (a different topic for each learner, to avoid them all queuing for the same resources and also to avoid unproductive collaboration).

5   **Train learners in the correct way to refer to source materials**. Make sure that in your own lectures and handouts, materials are referred to in the appropriate manner (for example: Bourner, T and Race, P (1991) *How to Win as a Part-time Student*, Kogan Page, London).

6   As well as helping learners develop individual skills to use libraries, **give them group exercises** (for example, tracking down relevant literature in preparation for a seminar). This allows learners to pick up library-use skills from each other.

7   **Remind learners that librarians are usually very willing to offer help and advice**, particularly when not simply being asked to do routine tasks such as finding a particular book. Often, subject librarians will not only have a detailed knowledge of the relevant stock in their subject, but will also have a good understanding of the subject itself, and can advise on which books and references are particularly worthwhile.

8   **Encourage learners to use their eyes!** For example, when there are several copies of a book on the shelves (or on the computer-catalogue listing) it is probable that the book is more useful than when only a single copy is stocked. Also, well-worn books (especially recent-yet-well-worn books) have obviously proved more useful than 'pristine' books.

9   Advise learners about **the other things they can use in libraries** besides books and journals. Many libraries contain a selection of audio-visual materials, computer-based learning packages and so on. Some have terminals linking to central computing facilities, and word-processing or desktop publishing systems which learners can book sessions on.

10   Many learners find that they work best in places such as libraries, away from other distractions. **Ensure that your learners know of the availability of study-spaces (and carrels)** and of the opening times of libraries (for example, late evenings and weekends, when there may be more space to spread out books and papers and easier access to stock).

34

Preparing interesting handouts

With modern developments in desktop publishing, coupled to the ready availability of photocopiers and offset litho printing, the use of handout materials has escalated dramatically. There is still, however, the danger that handout material is simply filed away and not used for active learning. Some ways round this are suggested below.

1   **Make handouts look attractive**. Gone are the days when a plain handwritten or typed summary of a lecture was enough. The quality of the message is now inextricably associated with the quality of the medium; scrappy handouts tend not to be valued.

2   **Use plenty of headings**. There's little more off-putting than a solid page of unbroken text. Where possible, make headings stand out by using bold print, or large-size print. When a glance at a handout gives information about the structure of its contents, it has already started to help people learn.

3   **Use white space**. For learners to develop a sense of ownership of handouts, they need to have room to write their own notes on them. Space between paragraphs, space at the top and bottom of pages, or a wide margin on one side are all ways of giving them this possibility of ownership.

4   **Use the start of a handout to remind learners what its purposes are**. It can be useful to explain the learning objectives of the particular element of work involved.

5   **Make handouts interactive**. In other words, include tasks and activities for learners to do, either in the group session where the handout was issued, or as later follow-up activities. (We've included on page 84 an example of an overhead transparency we use, highlighting the benefits of interactive handouts.)

6 **Include 'committed space' for learners to do things in handouts**. Structured tasks are best, such as, 'think of six reasons why the economy is in recession and list them below'. The fact that space has been provided for learners' answers helps persuade them (often subconsciously) to have a try at the tasks rather than simply skip them.

7 **Use tasks as chances for learners to learn by doing and to learn by getting things wrong**. Multiple-choice questions are useful for this. The handout can serve as a useful reminder of 'wrong' options chosen, as well as a pleasant reminder of 'correct' choices.

8 Use handouts to **avoid the wasteful process** of learners simply writing down things you say, or things they see on the screen or board. Copying things down is a low-level learning activity. Having such information already in handout form allows you to spend face-to-face time probing into the meaning of the information, interpreting it, questioning it, extrapolating from it, analysing it and so on.

9 Decide on **additions** that learners should make to their copies of the handout as the face-to-face session proceeds. For example, leave spaces for individual 'brainstorms' (eg, 'list five symptoms of anae-mia'), and for the products of buzz-group discussions (eg, putting some factors in order of importance). The aim should be that the handout learners take away at the end of the session is much more valuable than the 'blank' one they were given at the start. This also avoids learners simply asking for copies of the handout instead of participating in the session.

10 **Where possible, get your handout materials stored on disc in a desktop publishing or word-processing system**. It is then easy to make considerable adjustments and additions to handouts each successive time you use them.

Some advantages of interactive handouts

- **keep people active – and learning**
- **use learners' knowledge and experience**
- **show them how well they're learning (or not learning)**
- **help overcome language problems**
- **enable people to test out assumptions**
- **eliminate passive listening and note-copying**
- **ensure a good set of notes for later revision**
- **create psychological ownership**
- **cover more ground more rapidly for faster learners**
- **give opportunities for slower learners to digest and seek help**

More learning and less boredom during lectures

An overhead transparency, listing some of the advantages of making handout materials interactive.

Part 5

Various Kinds of Assessment

Our emphasis here is on ways of letting learners in on the 'secrets' of assessment criteria, and developing self-assessment and peer-assessment as ways of deepening the quality of their learning. We also include some suggestions for helping learners cope with more traditional forms of assessment.

35

Sharing assessment criteria

When learners are familiar with assessment criteria, they are better able to perform in ways which they know will meet the criteria. Teachers necessarily develop considerable expertise in assessment, but this expertise is not often shared with the learners.The following suggestions can help learners gain familiarity with – and confidence in – the rules of the game of assessment.

1　**Show learners marking schemes** from examinations and coursework assignments and explain exactly how the criteria are applied to typical specimen answers. Help them to see where marks are gained. Particularly address examples of where marks would be lost.

2　**Issue learners with marking criteria to apply to their own work**. Give them the opportunity to learn about their strengths and weaknesses by assessing samples of their work. Act as an expert witness when they are unsure about the interpretation of the marking criteria in the particular context of their own answers.

3　**Issue learners with assessment criteria to apply to each other's work**. Encourage them not simply to 'swap' their work with friends, but to continue to exchange work until no one knows who is assessing any piece of work. Act as an expert witness during the peer-assessment, helping with the interpretation of the criteria in the light of particular candidates' answers.

4　**Help learners to brainstorm a set of assessment criteria** for a particular piece of work they have done (or are about to do). Alternatively, take in examples of work done by previous students and get learners to devise criteria based on good and bad examples of past work. Help them re-phrase each of the criteria into words which they can apply with a minimum of uncertainty. Ask them to give relative weights to each of the criteria (for example, by asking them to apportion 30 points among 8 criteria) and then in due course arrange for them to apply their criteria to their own or each other's work.

5   Show learners an exam question or coursework question **and facilitate their production of a set of assessment criteria for the question**. Issue to the learners (in groups) a selection of good, poor and intermediate specimen answers to the question, and allow the learners to assess each example. Discuss in plenary the findings, explaining where necessary how particular criteria should have been applied to the respective specimens and exploring the score or grade each specimen should have been awarded.

6   Where learners have self-assessed or peer-assessed their own work, **act as a moderator**. Collect in the learner-marked work and check that the assessment has been done objectively. Write feedback comments as necessary about the quality of assessment and return to the learners who did the assessing.

7   **Ask learners (in groups) to design an examination or coursework assignment for an area they have studied**. Ask them to assign marks to each question and question part. Then ask them to write out a marking schedule for their examination or assignment and, where necessary, to re-adjust the questions so that the answers could be more objectively assessed. In plenary, act as expert witness showing how typical examiners may address the assessment of a selection of the questions the learners generated.

8   Where learners have participated in self- or peer-assessment, **ask them each to write down things they learned from the experience of applying assessment criteria**. Draw from the learners a list of their experiences. This normally shows that the act of assessing is in itself a highly productive way of learning about a subject.

9   **Encourage learners in groups or pairs to design tasks for each other and assessment criteria for each task**. Ask the learners to do the tasks and peer-assess each other's work using the criteria they designed. Ask the learners then to explain to each other exactly how the work was assessed. Act as troubleshooter in cases where particular learners feel that criteria were unfair, or assessment was not objective.

10   Give learners an example of an examination answer or coursework assignment answer **and ask them to (subjectively) give it an 'impression mark'** out of (say) 20 marks, recording their scores. Then guide them through an objective assessment of the sample, and discuss particular differences between the subjective scores and the objective ones.

36

Designing assessment criteria and performance indicators

Many of the difficulties learners have regarding formal assessment processes can be attributed to their lack of knowledge about 'the rules of the game'. The following suggestions describe ways of helping learners gain 'inside knowledge' of such rules.

1   When describing to learners course aims and objectives, give **illustrations** of the ways they will be expected to demonstrate their achievement of the objectives. For example, use past exam questions as case-studies, showing which objectives are involved in the questions and explaining to them the criteria against which achievement of the objectives has been measured.

2   It is increasingly common to use **competence statements** as devices to illustrate to learners the intended learning outcomes of a course. It is particularly helpful to learners to amplify competence statements by giving descriptions which help them to see exactly what standard of competence they should aim to deliver in due course.

3   **Help learners develop a frame of reference regarding standards.** Performance indicators can be used to show them what would constitute a satisfactory performance level and what additional requirements would be expected for the performance level to be 'good' and 'excellent'.

4   **Use past examples of learners' work** (essays, reports, videos of presentations and so on) to illustrate to learners different levels of performance. Examples can be very useful to bridge the gap between the standards that are required and 'what it actually looks like' when the standards are achieved.

5   Get learners in groups to work out assessment criteria which could be used to mark or grade **past examples** of essays and reports. It is useful to divide learners into groups for this, and ask each group to prepare a checklist of suggested criteria for the piece of work concerned. The different criteria emerging from respective groups of learners can then form the basis for a fruitful discussion about which criteria may be the most important and appropriate ones.

6   When setting learners tasks (essays, assignments, projects, seminar preparation, reports), **spend time giving clear suggestions about what should constitute a good end-product**. Though there is some danger that this is seen as 'spoon-feeding' learners, there is evidence that the more aware learners are of the expected outcomes, the higher is the standard of the work they produce.

7   When time permits, **allow learners themselves to work out suggested assessment criteria for tasks they are about to undertake**. Then help them to structure the criteria into a sensible pattern – one which may in due course be used to measure their work (either in tutor-assessed mode, or involving self-assessment or peer-assessment).

8   Give learners practice at **applying assessment criteria** to past examples of work. For example, get them to generate some criteria for an essay question, then ask them to apply the criteria to two or three actual essays. This clarifies exactly what is required to measure up to particular criteria and helps learners measure up to such criteria in their own future work.

9   Suggest to learners that it is useful for them to collect together a **'bank' of assessment criteria and performance indicators** for the various components of their course. Advise them that such a bank can be made much more effectively where groups of learners work together, sharing ideas and interpreting how criteria may best be worded.

10   In your own assessing (examinations and coursework), where possible **publish the actual assessment criteria** you employed (particularly when it was possible to generate the criteria with the learners themselves).

37

Giving learners written feedback

Written feedback from you can be regarded by learners as very authoritative. This has advantages and disadvantages. The following suggestions may help ensure that your feedback is received well by your learners.

1   Remember that when learners receive their work back, covered with feedback comments from you, **their feelings may be quite heightened**. In other words, they can be particularly sensitive to the feedback they receive, especially the first few comments they read.

2   Where a score or a grade is given, **this can dominate learners' reactions**. If the score is high, they may be pleased – but not read the feedback in any detail. If the score is low, they may be dispirited – and not read the feedback at all! Decide whether the score is important, or whether it would be better to give feedback without a score.

3   Remind yourself that the primary purposes of giving learners tutor-marked work is to let them find out exactly **how they are doing and what to do about any weak areas.**

4   **Think about the effect red ink has on learners**. Even when an excellent essay or report is returned covered with red comments (however positive) there is an instinctive anxiety on seeing 'all the red' on the script. This anxiety can get in the way of receiving feedback in a calm, objective way.

5   Easy as it is to insert crosses (beside errors or wrong answers), **crosses can be strongly demotivating to learners**. Crosses may bring back unhappy memories of schooldays. Similarly, it is all too easy to put ticks beside correct answers or ideas, when phrases such as 'good point', 'well done', 'nicely put', 'the hub of your argument', give pleasure to learners along with real feedback.

6   Consider using a **fluorescent highlighter pen** to mark incorrect phrases or words in scripts, rather than crossing them out, or underlining them, or ringing them. Margin notes or footnotes can add explanations relating to the highlighted words or phrases, so that learners can quickly tell exactly what you're getting at.

7   Where longer feedback comments and explanations are needed, **prepare a separate feedback sheet** with numbered points referring to identified parts of the marked work. A more structured way of giving more detailed feedback is to prepare assignment-return sheets listing the assessment criteria, giving these sheets out when setting the assignment, and returning them completed with your comments with the marked assignment.

8   Save yourself time and provide even more feedback by **preparing model answers to questions and assignments**, with your own commentary showing typical dangers and key points. You can then link particular comments on individual assignments to the model answers, saving you having to repeatedly write out explanations to common difficulties.

9   When providing a summary of feedback comments (such as an overall review of a piece of work), **try to start *and finish* with something positive**. Remember that learners' feelings will 'sink' with words such as 'however' (and plummet with phrases such as 'you've failed to grasp the basics'!).

10   For feedback to be really effective, it needs to reach learners **as fast as possible**, while their ideas are still fresh in their minds. Since it is impossible to mark a large pile of scripts straight away, one way of compensating for an inevitable delay regarding feedback is to issue model answers and commentaries immediately after learners hand in their work for assessment. This gives them instant general feedback and you can then prepare particular feedback with less urgency.

38

Giving learners verbal feedback

Giving verbal feedback to learners has both advantages and disadvantages over giving them written feedback. Below we present some ideas to help learners gain maximum benefit from verbal feedback.

1   It is useful to bear in mind that **learners may feel quite tense** when receiving verbal feedback from tutors. They may see tutors as both experts and figures of authority. The additional tension this can create can cause them to receive feedback in a somewhat distorted way, extrapolating beyond reason both the actual words and the manner in which you give them feedback.

2   Verbal feedback processes can convey more information than written feedback, since you have **tone of voice, facial expression and body language** to add to the words you choose to use.

3   **A problem with verbal feedback is that it is transient**. It is not easy for learners to reflect accurately on the feedback they receive face-to-face, as they tend to remember particular parts of it better than others.

4   The reactions of learners to verbal feedback can depend a lot on their **states of mind at the time of receiving the feedback**. If they are feeling positive and optimistic, they may remember mainly the positive things you say, while if they are feeling apprehensive they may remember mainly the critical comments you offer.

5   An advantage of verbal feedback processes is that they are normally **interactive**. You can observe what effects the words you use are having, and add further explanations when it is clear that your message is not yet getting across.

6   Think carefully about whether to give particular sorts of verbal feedback to learners **individually, or in groups.** Some learners can be embarrassed when they receive feedback (either positive or critical) in a group situation. It is probably safer to use group situations for more general feedback (for example, discussing common misconceptions or errors) and to save highly specific feedback for one-to-one feedback opportunities.

7   When you have a lot of verbal feedback to give to a group of learners, **it is useful to make notes in advance,** to save you having to remember on-the-spot the particular feedback messages you intend to give to each learner. It is sometimes useful to prepare these notes in a form where learners can take them away from the feedback exchange, serving them as an *aide-mémoire* when they reflect further on the feedback.

8   It can be frustrating for learners if they are eager to talk to you to gain some detailed feedback, but keep coming to seek you when you're elsewhere. It can be useful to pin a sheet of paper to your door, listing two or three slots when **you know you will be available** and asking learners to 'book themselves an appointment' by writing their names on the sheet and the time they intend to come to see you.

9   **Sometimes verbal feedback will be 'hard' on learners.** When you know this will be the case, try to find something positive to tell them about their work, particularly at the beginning of the interview – and maybe also at the very end.

10   One of the main advantages of giving feedback verbally is that you can estimate **the effect it is having** (which is much harder to do with written feedback). You can monitor learners' facial expressions and, if they seem to be over-sensitive to critical comment, you have the opportunity to soften your approach accordingly.

39

Preparing learners for peer-assessment

Peer-assessment allows learners to gain a great deal more feedback than they could gain just from their tutors. Moreover, the acts of working out assessment criteria and using them to measure each other's performance, help deepen learners' understanding of the work they assess. The following suggestions may help you maximize the benefits your learners can derive from engaging in peer-assessment.

1   **Take care not to impose peer-assessment on your learners** against their will. Accept that there will be at least some learners who regard it as your duty to do the assessing yourself. It is therefore necessary to spend some time helping them to appreciate that there are very powerful benefits they can gain from peer-assessment – particularly a deeper learning experience.

2   Show learners **how useful it is for them** to become more familiar with assessment criteria, increasing their ability to prepare themselves for formal assessments such as exams. Peer-assessment is a good way of helping them understand not only how assessment criteria are formulated, but also how they are applied in practice.

3   **Choose with care the task that is to be peer-assessed**. Try to find something where it will be particularly advantageous for learners to get feedback from each other and where a high level of specific expertise is not necessary to apply assessment criteria. Presentations, essays, reports, dissertations, posters and displays all lend themselves to peer-assessment if the conditions are appropriate.

4   The most important factors which determine the success (or otherwise) of peer-assessment are the **clarity and objectivity of the assessment criteria**. 'Interesting', 'stimulating', 'coherent' and 'well-structured' are terms which require additional descriptive detail if they are to be clear enough in everyone's mind to be used objectively as parts of assessment criteria.

5   Where possible, **minimize the feeling of 'risk'** which learners may feel regarding being measured by each other. For example, if the final scores only count for a small fraction of the coursework total, the feeling of risk is reduced. Alternatively, it could be agreed that the peer-assessment would be done purely as a learning experience (ie, scores would not 'count') – though then learners will not engage in it so seriously.

6   When possible, **allow the learners themselves to generate the assessment criteria**, and agree as a group on the weighting of each criterion (as well as agreeing on what each criterion will actually mean in practice). When learners have a sense of ownership of the criteria, they apply them more diligently than when they use other people's criteria.

7   **Ensure that there are not too many criteria** For example, learners peer-assessing each other's presentations can do so very well when using half-a-dozen criteria, but it would get much too complex if they tried to use 20 criteria simultaneously.

8   **It helps to prepare a grid**, with a list down the left-hand side of the 'agreed criteria', a column showing the 'score' given to each criterion, and columns for learners to enter their mark for each successive piece of work being assessed. After all the assessments have been completed, the grids can be collected in, averages computed and rank orders decided.

9   Help learners to appreciate that while the averaged results will give them useful information, **it is unproductive to challenge particular 'low' or 'high' scores in a personal way**. If the group of learners is very 'robust', however, it can be interesting to ask members of the group to justify why they awarded particularly high or low scores.

10   One of the most significant benefits that learners draw from peer-assessment is the **quantity of feedback** they receive. They can get much more feedback from a group of their peers than they would have been able to get from one 'expert witness' – the tutor. Having the tutor act as an 'ordinary' member of the group, giving scores in the same way as everyone else, combines the benefits of 'abundant' feedback and 'authoritative' feedback.

40

Preparing learners for self-assessment

It has been said that anyone who needs an assessor is not adequately prepared for the 'real world'. Self-assessment is a useful transferable skill and can be cultivated by using it as an integral part of courses.

1   Help learners to see the usefulness of measuring their own work as a way of **looking more deeply at things they have done** and enhancing their understanding of subjects and concepts.

2   Advise learners that the most important aspects of self-assessment are not the actual grades or scores which learners may award themselves. Much more important are the **opportunities to reflect** on work they have done and the chance to think about the nature of assessment criteria related to the work.

3   It is easy to dismiss the use of self-assessment because of suspicions that learners 'will be kind to themselves' and will rate their own work over-generously. While it is true that *some* learners may do this, it is usual for learners on average to be rather **'harder'** when self-assessing their work than tutors would be.

4   It is useful to **help learners to generate the criteria** that they subsequently employ during self-assessment. The greater the feeling of ownership learners have over such criteria, the more objectively they will apply them.

5   **A useful way of generating criteria** to be used in self-assessment is to ask each learner to write down, for example, 'features of a successful report'. Then get learners into groups of three or four, and ask each group to shortlist the four most important features. Ask the groups to then turn each 'feature' into a checklist question which would determine whether the feature had been adequately demonstrated (ie, into assessment criteria). Ask each group for its most important checklist question and compile a list of a dozen or so such criteria. From such a list, discuss and agree on the most useful of the criteria which have emerged.

6   Whereas with peer-assessment it is necessary for everyone involved to be using the same set of criteria, with self-assessment there is **room for manoeuvre**. For example, five 'core' criteria could be agreed, which everyone would use in the self-assessment, but a further three 'additional' criteria could be left to each individual to formulate. These 'additional' criteria could then be formulated specially to take into account individual approaches to the task to be self-assessed.

7   Where assessment marks or scores are to contribute to the formal assessment profile of learners, it may be necessary to involve tutors in **a 'moderating' role**. For example, tutors could themselves assess the pieces of work and if the respective assessments were significantly different (eg, by more than 5 per cent) negotiations could take place to decide an agreed grade or score. In practice, it is only in about one case in ten where such negotiations prove to be needed.

8   Acting as a moderator in self-assessment processes can be far easier than assessing work 'from scratch'. **It is much quicker to 'skim' work**, checking whether agreed assessment criteria have been self-applied objectively, than to apply the criteria 'from cold'. Self-assessment can therefore save tutors' time – particularly important when large numbers of learners are involved.

9   Probably the most useful contributions tutors can make to self-assessment processes is to give learners feedback on the **quality of their self-assessment**. This feedback progressively leads learners to more objective self-assessment.

10 It is to be expected that a small minority of learners will regard it as 'a right' to receive **tutor-assessment** and will object in principle to being asked to self-assess their work. If they remain unconvinced by explanations of how they can benefit from self-assessment, it is best to defer to their wishes and provide such learners with traditional tutor-assessment. It is important that the group as a whole is not allowed to feel that the use of self-assessment is any kind of 'abdication from duty' on the part of tutors.

A peer-assessment grid

Criteria	Weight	A	B	C	D	E	F	G	H
1									
2									
3									
4									
5									
6									
7									
8									
Total									

An example of a grid which can be used by each learner in a group, where they all peer-assess eight examples of work (eg, presentations) against a set of agreed criteria.

A self-assessment grid

Agreed Criteria	weight	score	Comments
Idiosyncratic Criteria			
Total			

An example of a grid which learners can use to self-assess their own work against some agreed criteria, with space for individual learners to identify additional criteria with particular relevance to their individual approaches to the task.

41

Negotiating learning agreements

A useful way of empowering learners and of giving them a greater sense of ownership of their learning is to help them to negotiate learning agreements. The following steps can be helpful in such processes.

1   Convince learners that it is useful and beneficial for them to have the **additional flexibility and control which they gain by negotiating learning agreements**. This can also give them a greater degree of choice over the detailed nature of their studies.

2   **Learning agreements can be negotiated in different ways**. For example, a detailed proposal can be drawn up by each learner and then used as the basis for a single negotiation with a tutor, the outcome of which is a negotiated agreement. Alternatively, the negotiations can be staged and successive elements of the agreement progressively approved, such as the objectives, the processes to be used, the timescale and the products.

3   While the most significant parts of negotiated learning agreements usually involve tutor–learner negotiations, remind learners how useful it can be to **practise negotiating with each other**, as a way of preparing themselves for the ways in which they will present their proposals at the 'real' negotiation session.

4   Negotiated learning agreements lend themselves both to agreements between a tutor and each single learner, and also to agreements between one or more tutors and a **group of learners**. Group agreements may be rather more complex if it is also necessary to assess in some way the respective contributions of each member of the group to the final product the group delivers.

5   Explain to learners that the most important starting-point for any learning agreement is a clear, detailed **set of objectives**. From the objectives it can be seen whether the level of the work to be completed is appropriate and realistic. The objectives should also make it clear exactly why the work is being structured in the ways chosen.

6   Having worked out a set of objectives, the logical next step is to summarize the **processes** which will be used to achieve each objective. Encourage learners to think of more than one way each objective could be achieved, so that in the process of negotiating the learning agreement, it can be decided which approaches are the most recommendable ones.

7   Having decided on the objectives and the processes, the next important decision is to place a **timescale** on the work involved. Encourage learners to set interim deadline proposals for various stages of the work they plan to do, rather than simply setting themselves a final deadline.

8   The remaining important element of negotiations is the **form in which the product of the learning agreement will be delivered**. There are all sorts of possibilities, ranging from written reports, seminar presentations, production of a video, demonstration of a software program and so on. When negotiating a range of agreements with a large group of learners, it becomes necessary for tutors to give some guidance on the format the product should take, otherwise some learners may well spend an inordinate amount of time developing products which are highly advanced.

9   It is useful to use the negotiation session to devise **assessment criteria** for the products of the work. These criteria can normally be closely related to the objectives of the work.

10   It can be useful to negotiate-in a certain amount of **flexibility**. For example, an agreement can incorporate processes for an accepted amount of renegotiation, for circumstances where it becomes clear while carrying out the agreed work that additional or different aspects should be investigated further.

42

Helping learners revise productively

If learners worked steadily throughout their studies, there would be no need for the more concentrated work known as 'revision'. However, it would appear that human nature dictates that the need for revision is inevitable. Learners often adopt revision techniques which are far from productive. Exams measure the quality of revision even more than the quantity of revision. The following suggestions can help learners focus their energies effectively.

1   Suggest that learners start revision **really early** – as soon as they have something they can revise. Point out how much more enjoyable – and efficient – revision is when there is no exam threatening.

2   **Give learners lots of questions to practise with**. Exams primarily measure learners' ability to answer questions, so such practice is one of the most relevant activities learners preparing for exams can engage in.

3   **Get learners to formulate lists of questions for themselves** to practise with. Some help regarding what sort of question is useful may be required. Questions which learners have formulated them-selves are 'owned' by the learners and their efforts to become able to answer such questions are enhanced considerably.

4   **Show learners exactly how their exam papers will be structured**. When learners know what kinds of questions to expect, they can focus their preparations to answer them. Give learners the chance to apply assessment criteria to their own (and each other's) work. The act of assessing helps them remember criteria of the sort they need in due course to live up to.

5   **Help learners to think about their own learning styles,** for example, 'visual', 'aural', 'reading/writing' and 'kinetic'. Help them to make their own range of revision aids for each of the ways they like to learn, for example, posters for visual learning, audiotapes for listeners, summary and quiz cards for 'reading/writing' learners, and collaborative programmes for 'kinetic' learning.

6   **Encourage learners to quiz each other**. This can be more productive (and less intimidating) than working on their own. It also allows learners the opportunity to learn by explaining things to each other.

7   **Alert learners to the dangers of passive reading**. Remind them how easy it is to read something time and time again, but still not become able to apply it. Revision should only be considered productive if some writing activity is in progress, or when practising answering questions in one way or another.

8   **Encourage learners to make 'tight' summaries of information**. The act of summarizing helps them prioritize their subject matter and a collection of good summaries helps reduce the task of revision to manageable proportions.

9   **Suggest that learners revise in frequent, short spells,** rather than long continuous ones. Concentration spans last minutes rather than hours! There's no point sitting for hours on end if no learning payoff is accruing.

10   **Encourage learners to bring variety to their revision**. Frequent changes of subject matter increase learning payoff. Sticking with each topic for no more than half an hour at a time is a useful ground rule. A change is as good as a rest – and much more productive.

43

Helping learners pass exams

Whatever exams are intended to measure, the one certainty is that they measure learners' abilities to answer exam questions. The suggestions below outline some ways of developing learners' abilities to answer exam questions logically and successfully.

1   **Help learners gain familiarity with the appearance and structure of exam papers**. In this context, familiarity breeds confidence. When learners are used to the appearance of exam papers, there is less chance that they will react in a tense, disorganized manner in their exams. Let them see examples of exam questions very early in their course so they know what to expect later regarding the general standards they should aim to meet.

2   **Allow learners to apply assessment criteria to good – and bad – examples of candidates' answers**. Learners are quick to learn exactly where marks can be lost – or gained.

3   **Emphasize the importance of good time-management in exams**. Point out the logic that if learners attempt (for example) only two-thirds of the paper, their maximum possible score is only 66 per cent. Exams measure time-management as well as knowledge.

4   **Give learners practice at analysing exam questions**. Ask them to decide exactly what each question requires – and what it does not require. Help learners identify the key words in exam questions, notably 'why?', 'how?', 'what?', 'when?', 'compare', 'discuss', 'explain', 'give an example of ...' and so on.

5   When learners have a choice of questions, **point out how important it is for them to make their choices sensibly**. The best way to do this is to read each question in turn slowly, calmly – and more than once. Only then is it possible to make an informed choice regarding which questions to attempt.

6   **Encourage learners to re-read each question several times while answering it.** Point out that more marks are lost in exams by learners 'going off at a tangent' than for any other single cause. Frequent re-reading of the questions can prevent tangents altogether. Suggest that every 15 minutes or so, they ask themselves, 'Am I answering the question?'

7   **Stress the importance in numerical or problem-type questions of showing the examiners exactly how an answer is reached.** If examiners can see exactly where an error occurred, they can give due credit for all the parts of the answer which were correctly attempted. Conversely, if examiners can only see the 'wrong' answer, they can't give any marks at all.

8   When learners get 'stuck' because something won't come back to mind, encourage them to **move to some other question they can answer well.** Leaving a gap and moving on is better than sitting getting into a panic. What matters is scoring points on the whole paper, not getting a particular question absolutely right.

9   **Help learners to see that examiners are human.** Examiners like to be able to award marks – they are not simply searching for mistakes! Examiners respond best to clear, well laid-out answers.

10   Point out the benefits of saving some time towards the end of each exam for **a complete re-reading of the script**. Learners can pick up many extra marks as they re-read, by correcting obvious errors and adding any important further details which have surfaced in their minds since they wrote their answers.

What do exams really measure? An agenda

How much you know?

How much you don't know?

How fast you can write?

How good your memory is?

How much work you did the night before?

How well you keep your cool?

How competent you are?

How well you can read the questions?

How good you are at answering exam questions?

How *practised* you are at answering exam questions?

How you perform under pressure?

How good you are at time-management?

How well you can keep addressing the question?

How *often* you've practised on similar questions?

How well you read your own answers?

An overhead transparency we use when helping learners think about revision and exams.

Part 6

Life Skills

In this final section, we give some general suggestions covering some of the skills learners will need throughout their careers and, particularly, some skills they will need when looking for employment.

44

Helping learners cope with being away from home

The first experience of taking full responsibility for life away from home is probably even more important to many learners than their studies. Perhaps this is where their *education* begins (not just their training). The following suggestions may help you help them.

1   Accept that for many learners, being away from home for the first extended time is a cause of both **stress and excitement**. Acknowledge that at times their full attention will not be on their studies in general, or on your subject in particular.

2   In a lecture or tutorial near the start of the course, give some time to a group task in which learners list both the **benefits** of the experience of living away from home and the **drawbacks** associated with being away from home.

3   Ask learners to work out the **positive learning experiences** which can be drawn from adapting to living away from home and explore how these learning experiences can transfer productively to later developments in their education and careers.

4   **Help learners to form self-help groups**, where they can gain mutual support and advice regarding any problems they encounter because of the changes they experience living away from home.

5   Suggest that groups of learners invite some final-year learners as **'expert witnesses'**, to share ways and means that they used to adapt to living away from home.

6   **Encourage learners to find a mentor** and also to be mentors to each other. Help them to work out role-descriptions for mentors and to address the benefits that can be gained by mentors as well as by 'mentees'.

7   One problem of being away from home is the danger of losing friends by failing to keep in contact. Suggest that a **very short letter** is often enough to keep channels of communication open – or even a postcard, or a word-processor-produced 'round robin'.

8   Point out the danger of **putting off** corresponding with (or telephoning) contacts at home, while waiting 'until things have settled down, and I have something definite to report'. In the fast-moving experiences of higher education, things are unlikely to ever 'settle down'.

9   **Encourage learners to tune in to their new locations** and develop new roots in the new environment. Suggest they join relevant local clubs and societies. Perhaps they can set up some social events with the local population.

10   **Establish helplines or remind learners of existing channels of help** such as counsellors, advisers, personal tutors. Encourage learners to seek out such people even when they have no particular worries, simply to get to know them. (To a counsellor, a meeting with a learner *without* a problem is a pleasant change!)

45

Helping learners cope with stress

Few people have not had to cope with stress at one time or another. Many people seem to cope with long-term continual stress. Stress can be felt more deeply by people who are coping with it for what seems to them like 'the first time' – this includes many learners in higher education.

1   **Help learners to accept that stress is a natural part of life**. It does not help at all simply to rail at the situation or allocate blame.

2   Convince learners that every stressful situation can be viewed as a **useful learning experience**. Coping with stress – or even temporarily 'going under' due to stress – can both be used to build up coping strategies.

3   **Help learners decide when they are stressed**. Point out that a person who is highly stressed may not realize this. It often takes other people to see that someone is over-stressed. Encourage learners to talk to each other about how they feel and to be willing to advise each other when symptoms of over-stress are evident.

4   Remind learners that a certain amount of stress is actually **healthy**. Adrenalin levels can be raised a little and performance can be improved. The only time to worry about stress is when it gets in the way of a balanced and enjoyable life, or when it starts to have repercussions on other people.

5   Encourage learners who feel they may be stressed **to use any or all of the avenues of help open to them**. Counsellors, chaplains, course tutors, doctors, advisers and fellow-learners can all provide tangible help to people who are over-stressed.

6   Sometimes the best time to address the topic of stress is when one is completely unstressed. It can therefore be quite useful to attend **a session on stress-management without** any particular reason for attending, simply as a learning experience to store for later use if needed.

7   Encourage learners to **exchange their own experiences** at coping with stressful situations. Many find particular hobbies or relaxation techniques serve them well and can introduce the techniques to others.

8   Other people are often blamed for causing stress. In fact, of course, there is little anyone can do to alter how other people behave. It is usually much more productive to consider altering **how one reacts to other people's behaviour**. Therefore, advising learners to retain ownership of how they react to stressful situations is more useful than trying to find ways of changing each situation for them.

9   **Many kinds of stress are avoidable**. For example, the stress many learners feel during intensive revision can be avoided by planning the revision well, starting it early and doing it less intensively. Suggest to learners ways of identifying in advance future stress situations and acting early to minimize the stresses.

10 One of the biggest stress factors in many learners' minds is the possibility of **failure**. Encourage learners likely to be *over-stressed* about possible failure to regard failure as simply a **temporary** – if inconvenient – setback, and an experience which itself provides useful learning experiences.

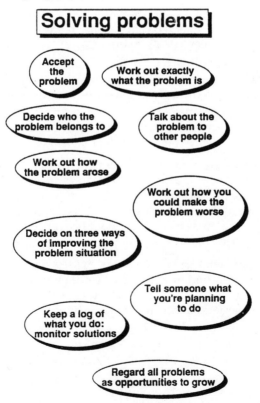

46

Recovering from two weeks off

Most learners will, at some point in their studies, need to take time off due to circumstances quite beyond their control (illness, bereavement in the family, personal problems and so on). With large groups, it can be difficult to know when help is needed and how to provide such help. The following suggestions may assist.

1   Create mechanisms where learners who need to take time off **alert you** to the fact. Checking up who misses tutorials can be one way of finding out who may have a problem. Keep records so that you find out (and can offer to help) before any learner may have dropped out for too long.

2   Create a climate where learners who know of fellow-learners with problems feel that they can **alert tutors** to the situation. When it is clear that you're not simply being dogmatic about attendance at lectures and seminars, learners are usually willing to alert tutors to any real difficulties they know their colleagues are facing.

3   **Build up a collection of resources** you can give out to learners who have missed important sessions. Copies of your own lecture notes may be useful. Questions, problems and case-studies which were dealt with in the missed sessions are likely to be particularly useful. References to textbooks which would cover the missed sessions will also be useful.

4   For learners who have necessarily missed part of their studies, it is particularly important that they feel they can **ask questions** about anything they can't understand as they try to catch up on their own. Give the learners concerned a definite time and place to approach you with any problems they have.

5   Encourage learners who have missed something important to **use their fellow-learners as a resource**. Explain to the whole group that it is a very useful learning experience to explain something one has just learned. The act of putting it into words to explain it is a good way of understanding it oneself.

6   Show learners who have missed something how it is better to **keep up with what is going on now**, rather than to spend all their time trying to catch up on what they missed and thus continuing to remain behind. Suggest they catch up 'a bit at a time' while continuing with the work being done in class at present.

7   Where learners have necessarily missed deadlines for coursework, it may be worth coming to **'special arrangements'** – for example, setting a deadline for a rough outline of the work to be submitted, with a later deadline for the final submission. This can allow you to be alerted to any significant problems which may have been caused by the time out. It is also better than allowing them to miss out altogether on the element of coursework concerned, with cumulative adverse effects at the end of the course or module.

8   Where possible, **build in choices and alternatives**, particularly regarding coursework (and also exam questions). When learners have such choices, it becomes less critical that they catch up on everything they may have missed.

9   When there is something that is crucial to your course, **devise alternative means** for those learners who may necessarily miss it. Alternatives include making a video of an important lecture (or even a simple audio tape), making a detailed handout, preparing a short open-learning package covering the topic, or providing a 'remedial' or 'repeat' session for people who did not 'get it' first time round.

10   **Help learners who have missed something to keep a sensible perspective**. One small point that is not 'understood' can seem like a mountain, when in fact is may not be significant at all. Remind learners that any problem is only a problem until they find out how to solve it.

47

Recovering from failure

Learners who have failed often feel that it's entirely their own fault and that they should not expect any help from their tutors. However, there is much that tutors can do to help learners recover from failure. The following suggestions may help you to help those learners who, for one reason or another, don't manage to succeed first time on your courses.

1   When learners have failed at something, **help them to accept it**. Running away from it may be an instinctive reaction, but it does not help them to prevent a similar thing happening in future. Once learners have accepted that a particular episode was unsuccessful, they can begin structured preparations to guarantee that it will be successful next time.

2   Help learners suffering from depression after failure **to look at the failure as a learning opportunity**. Point out how unimportant and fruitless it is for them to dwell on 'letting people down' feelings. Remind them that every successful person has recovered from failures at one time or another. Advise them to work out constructively exactly what they were not able to do.

3   Explain that 'failure' is a **transient stage**, when what the learners managed to do simply did not match what they were required to do at that stage. Having failed does not mean that they 'can't ever do it', it simply meant they 'couldn't yet do it' on a particular occasion.

4   Remind learners how useful it is for them to know exactly what they **can't yet** do. Only when they have this knowledge can they systematically fine-tune their learning to eliminate the possibility of the same thing going wrong in future.

5   Give examples of how 'getting something wrong' is one of the most **effective ways** of eventually getting it right. Knowing what can cause problems is useful knowledge for the future. In life in general, probably more is learned by getting it wrong at first, than by getting it right first time.

6   Encourage small groups of learners who have failed something to **work together** to find ways of analysing what caused the failure. Sharing problems with other learners in the same situation can be comforting.

7   Make sure that learners who have failed something **don't feel** *themselves* **to be failures!** An exam failure may seem daunting at the time, but it is only a very small and quite artificial measure of what a person can or can't do. Remind them that it is not themselves who are failures – it is simply a matter of something that at a particular time, and in particular circumstances, they did not manage to achieve.

8   Where learners need to prepare for a resit examination, encourage them to look not only at which parts of the subject caused them difficulties, but at their **approaches to learning** the subject. It often pays dividends to analyse study-skills such as revision and exam technique in the light of an unsuccessful episode.

9   Advise learners working for resit examinations that they may indeed find themselves **at an advantage** in the next stage of their studies. Other learners who did not need resits may have forgotten much of their previous knowledge when they return for the next part of their studies, while those who have done resits have it fresher in their minds (and maybe also have a deeper understanding due to the extra time they have spent studying and the analysis of past difficulties).

10 When learners move on after recovering from a failure, **help them keep track of their own progress**, so that they are better placed to self-assess their position. Sharing assessment criteria with learners in general can help. It can also be useful to ask learners to give a rough estimate of how they *feel* their studies are going, and what they may need to do to adjust their studying to bridge any gap between where they feel they are and where they intend to be.

48

Helping learners apply for jobs

Writing an effective CV is one part of making a good application for a job. Other important aspects include writing a suitable letter of application and, not least, filling in application forms themselves. Giving learners practice to help them develop these skills is a useful addition to other parts of their education.

1   Make a collection of good, bad and indifferent **letters of application** for posts and issue these to learners as a basis for discussion.

2   Get learners themselves to work out **criteria for a good letter of application**, using your assorted materials to identify strengths and weaknesses exemplified in them.

3   Ask learners themselves to draft letters of application for a fictitious post, experimenting with different approaches to the task. If possible, form a **'selection panel'** of colleagues (or learners from another group) and ask the panel to select what it considers are the best letters, identifying the features which caused these letters to be preferred.

4   Where learners need to become acquainted with desktop publishing or word-processing systems, help them develop a file of **'letter skeletons'** which can be used later to produce specific letters rapidly, by inserting the particular data relating to the post being applied for and specific comments to support the applications.

5   Collect a **range** of the sorts of application forms which learners may expect to meet from firms and organizations. It can be useful to make overhead transparencies of typical forms to use in illustrating the sorts of information learners will need to have to hand when dealing with such forms.

6   Remind learners of the importance of the **appearance** of submitted application forms. As it is not easily possible to use word-processing systems to deal with complex forms, greater care may need to be taken in typing information onto the forms. Remind learners that it may be worth their choosing to pay a skilled typist to prepare submission copies of important application forms.

7   Suggest to learners that however many applications they have in the pipeline, it's worth **retaining a photocopy** of each form they submit. Those application forms that lead to shortlisting will probably contain much of the information upon which interview questions will be based, so it becomes very useful to refer to the details put into the forms when preparing for interview.

8   Many application forms ask for quite 'deep' answers to questions. For example, they may have space for applicants to outline their career aims and ambitions. It is useful to give learners some **practice** at expressing these in a convincing and effective way.

9   Remind learners that even if they have not yet held any full-time employment posts, it may be well worth giving details of **vacation jobs** they have done, particularly when the jobs involved positions of responsibility or trust.

10 Encourage learners to use opportunities on their application forms to paint attractive pictures of them as **sociable human beings**. Employers are unlikely to wish to recruit 'loners' – however gifted academically. For example, leisure activities and hobbies can be a way of demonstrating that applicants are capable of collaborating with other people, for example in societies, clubs and so on.

49

Helping learners prepare CVs

Apart from obtaining degrees or diplomas successfully, preparing a good curriculum vitae is one of the most important activities that learners may do during a college course. There are many ways that you may be able to assist in this process, including those listed below.

1   Remind learners that their skills of **written communication** (and indeed layout and presentation) are vitally important in helping them to be shortlisted in job applications when they finish their studies.

2   **Show them a range of examples of CVs**. Ask them to make judgements based both on their first impressions of each CV and on more penetrating analysis.

3   Help learners decide on the **main sections** to include in an effective CV. For example, give them advice on the balance to be struck between sections such as 'general information', 'education and training', 'employment', 'career aims', 'leisure interests' and so on.

4   Ensure that somewhere in their programme of coursework, learners have the opportunity not only to prepare a CV but also to receive **detailed feedback on its effectiveness**.

5   Preparing a CV can be coupled with **information technology or word-processing development**. A useful end-product gives learners a genuine reason for increasing their skills at using word-processing or desktop publishing equipment. They may well need the skills they develop later, for example when writing project reports or dissertations.

6   Help learners to identify the **aims** they should have in mind when putting together a CV. For example, they should try to pave the way towards interview questions which they will answer with confidence (perhaps on leisure interests) and they should try to find ways of making their achievements and qualifications look impressive and convincing.

7   Remind learners that their CVs need to serve as **'ambassadors'** for them, giving an impression of well-organized, highly-motivated and interesting people. Therefore the structure of the pages and the style and presentation all have roles to play in getting them shortlisted for interview.

8   When it is possible to devote sufficient time to CV development, get learners to produce the best CV they can and then constitute a 'real' **selection panel** (maybe from another group of learners) to pick out a shortlist (and to give reasons explaining why selections were made and why other examples were not chosen).

9   Give learners encouragement to 'polish' their CVs **collaboratively**. The detailed feedback they can give each other while editing and refining their CVs can be very valuable. Try to overcome worries about the possibility that they will end up competing directly with each other for exactly the same posts at the end of their studies – statistically this is not nearly as likely as they may think.

10   When the time comes for learners to produce their CVs 'for real', they will appreciate **continued advice from you**. They may in any case wish you to be a referee for their applications and the more you already know about their CVs, the simpler your task of providing a focused reference may be.

50

Developing learners' interview skills

In the final analysis, however successful learners are academically, to secure a position they need to convince one or more people, face-to-face, that they're ideal for the post concerned. Interview skills (like most skills) can be learned by trial and error. However, there is much that tutors can do to minimize the 'error'.

1   Establish the importance of **face-to-face communication skills** in life in general. Remind learners that if other people are to be convinced by them, they often have to do the convincing face-to-face. Getting the job they really want may depend on giving a good interview.

2   Help learners to appreciate that face-to-face communication is learned best by **practice and trial-and-error**, but that much of the learning can be done in 'safe' situations such as role-play exercises with their peers.

3   Sometimes at interviews, candidates are requested to **'tell us a bit about yourself'**. Open-ended questions like this can be harder to deal with than direct questions. Use a tutorial or seminar session to allow each member of the group to give a short (three-minute) description of his or her education and background. The main purpose of this is simply to help learners become more comfortable when talking about themselves.

4   A trickier interview question is 'well, then, will you tell us exactly **why we should offer *you* the post?'**. Again, this is something that can be developed by practice. An appropriate balance between modesty and 'blowing one's own trumpet' is required and the feedback that learners can receive from each other (and from you) can be very useful in helping them to develop the right balance.

5   At an appropriate point in a course, a little before learners are setting out on the main task of job-hunting, it can be worth devoting some time (maybe a few tutorial or seminar slots) to an **on-going role-play scenario** as follows. First, get learners to produce CVs and application forms (for a fictitious post, for example), and set up interview panels with learners role-playing key personnel (training manager, managing director, personnel officer, recruitment manager) for a firm or organization.

6   Allow all learners to take part in the interviews, once as a candidate **and at least once role-playing some of the panel members**. Structure the interviews to be as close as possible to real-life scenarios, giving the panel members enough time to read the documentation from each 'candidate' and to prepare questions relevant to the roles they are playing. Have other members of the group as observers, taking notes of 'triumphs' and 'disasters' during the interviews.

7   Where possible, **use a television studio** for some of the interviews, with learners operating cameras and editing equipment. It is then possible for candidates to privately view the video of their interviews, learning a great deal from the experience with little need for anyone to talk them through their strengths and weaknesses!

8   **Play back videos of interviews** (maybe last year's interviews) to groups of learners and use them to generate lists of 'dos and don'ts' for interviews.

9   It is often possible to recruit some interested personnel from companies or organizations you have connections with to constitute some **'real' people for a selection panel**. Some firms may even provide a 'prize' (a working visit to the United States was provided by one firm we know) for the most successful candidate in the simulated interviews.

10   **Encourage learners to practise informally with each other**. Small syndicates can role-play interviews as a regular (entertaining) part of their social activities, gradually developing members' abilities to be comfortable when put on the spot and, most important, the confidence and 'coolness' which will eventually land them the posts they want.

And finally ... helping large groups of learners

Many of the ideas in this book relate to teaching large groups. More and more, tutors are finding themselves under growing pressure because of increases in the sizes of the classes on their courses. The following suggestions aim to help tutors cope with larger numbers of learners and to keep tutors' workloads to manageable proportions.

1   **Don't be frightened by big audiences**. Talking to a large audience becomes better with practice. In any case, learners are normally far more concerned with trying to make sensible notes and trying to understand your subject, than with judging your competence at addressing large groups.

2   **Split the group in two or four**. Not every timetabled slot needs to be a mass lecture. Save the mass lectures for things where the whole group really needs to be together and use the smaller groups for things where you need to be able to interact with members of the group.

3   **Take written questions**. Issue small slips of paper, or Post-its, and ask members of the large group to put their key questions in writing, for you to address at the next session. You can soon see what the most common questions are and spend a few minutes at the start of each large-group session dealing with the main issues arising from the questions. Large groups are usually very attentive when *their* questions are being dealt with.

4   **Keep your assessment load down**. With small groups, it may have been relatively easy for you to mark several pieces of work from each learner, but with larger groups it is advisable to concentrate on key pieces of work where learners really need *your* feedback. Some other pieces of work can be turned into self-assessment exercises, where learners self-check their work using a printed checklist or marking scheme, which you supply when they are ready to self-assess.

5   **Consider using peer-assessment formally**. It can be quicker to facilitate learners in a large group peer-assessing each other's work than if you were to assess all the work yourself. You can still act as *moderator*, taking in all the work and quickly checking that the assessment has been fair, or as *arbitrator* where particular learners believe that the peer-assessment has not been fair.

6   **Have a timetabled 'surgery' for each course**. Let learners know an hour when you will be available to discuss any problems they face. Remember to check that the large group has not any other timetabled activity at the time planned for your 'surgery'.

7   **Where possible, adopt a team-teaching approach**. If two or three colleagues are handling large-group sessions, it is much simpler to deal with emergencies such as illness.

8   **Consider 'structured' assessments**. For exams or tests, it is often possible to ask structured questions (multiple-choice, true/false, 'put these in the correct sequence', 'what's wrong with this diagram?' and so on), rather than open-ended questions. Structured questions are usually far quicker to mark, especially when you have large numbers of scripts.

9   **Get everything important down on paper**. Use handouts (or a course manual) to provide learners with all the key information they need, such as syllabus details, assessment schedules, key references, questions to practise on and so on. It is then much easier for learners who miss particular sessions to catch up without asking you endless questions.

10 **Be firm on deadlines for assessed coursework**. Publish the deadlines clearly in handouts and on notice-boards. Suggesting that work handed in after the deadline will be assessed out of 50 per cent rather than 100 per cent has a dramatic effect on punctuality of submission – and helps you control your marking-time better.

Further Reading

The books we have selected for this annotated bibliography are only a small cross-section of the vast literature on techniques and theories of education and training. They have been chosen because we find them useful and enjoy them – or because we know them rather well because we were involved in their creation! Where publications are from specialist small publishers, we have added contact addresses to make it easier for you to track them down.

Brown, G and Atkins, M (1988) *Effective Teaching in Higher Education* Routledge, London.
Based on meticulous research, this book also provides practical guidance and good ideas.

Brown, S (ed) (1991) *Students at the Centre of Learning* SCED Publications, Gala House, Birmingham, B5 7RA.
A collection of articles focusing on learning, and including discussions of peer-group learning, personal tutoring and learning contracts.

Brown, S and Baume D (eds) *Learning Contracts: Volume 1 (A Theoretical Perspective); Volume 2 (Some Practical Examples)* SCED Publications, Gala House, Birmingham, B5 7RA.
Two SCED Papers (71/72) bringing together a wide range of approaches to the development of learning contracts and learning agreements.

Bourner, T and Race, P (1991) *How to Win as a Part-Time Student* Kogan Page, London.
This book arose from the results of research into the needs and problems of part-time students. It is written in open-learning format, with self-analysis questions through-out the text and the authors' responses to each question collected together in the last part of the book.

Bourner, T, Martin, V and Race, P (1993) *Workshops that Work* McGraw Hill, Maidenhead.
This book was great fun to write! All three of the authors enjoy running 'active learning' training and education workshops in their own ways, and learned a great deal from each other while putting together their ideas for this book.

Gibbs, G and Jenkins, A (eds) *Teaching Large Classes in Higher Education* Kogan Page, London.
This book arose from a series of workshops conducted widely in the UK, funded by the Polytechnics and Colleges Funding Council (PCFC), and contains many of the best ideas from the booklets used to accompany the workshops, covering these ideas in greater detail.

Gibbs, G, Habeshaw and Habeshaw, T (1989) *53 Interesting Things to Do in Your Lectures* Technical and Educational Services, 37 Ravenswood Road, Bristol, BS6 6BW.
Gibbs, G, Habeshaw, S and Habeshaw, T (1992) *53 Interesting Ways to Teach Large Classes* Technical and Educational Services, 37 Ravenswood Road, Bristol, BS6 6BW.
Habeshaw, S, Habeshaw, T and Gibbs, G (1989) *53 Interesting Things to Do in Your Seminars and Tutorials* Technical and Educational Services, 37 Ravenswood Road, Bristol, BS6 6BW.
All these books (and the whole of the '53' series published by Technical and Educational Services) are useful providers of a wide range of ideas. The authors concentrate on a practical, learning-centred approach. It's best not to expect all 53 ideas in each book to be directly relevant to your work – but we doubt if there is anyone whose teaching won't benefit by trying out a few of the ideas. These books are the best-known parts of a rapidly growing collection (presently about 20 books in the series, covering a wide range of techniques and situations), and we suggest that readers may find out the latest about the series by writing to the Bristol address quoted.

Ellington, H I and Race, P (1993) *Producing Teaching Materials* Kogan Page, London.
Basically, this is a 'how to do it' book on the design, production and use of a wide range of teaching resources, ranging from how best to use a stick of chalk to computer conferencing as a means of developing students' communication skills.

Ellington, H I, Percival, F and Race, P (1993) *A Handbook of Educational Technology* Kogan Page, London.
This book is probably not so much about technology *in* education and training, but technology *of* education and training. It includes chapters on educational strategies, the use of objectives and competence descriptors, mass instruction, individualized learning and group learning.

McGill, I and Beaty, L (1992) *Action Learning – A Practitioner's Guide* Kogan Page, London.
Packed with ideas on ways of getting people to learn from each other, as well as by learning by doing.

Newble, D and Cannon, R (1991) *A Handbook for Teachers in Universities and Colleges* Kogan Page, London.
One of the friendliest books that we know of for teachers in colleges. The approach is practical and straightforward, and the handbook covers a very wide range of teaching and learning situations.

Race, P (1989) *The Open Learning Handbook* Kogan Page, London.
This book is addressed to those designing open learning resource materials, and to tutors supporting learners on flexible learning programmes. A second edition is presently being planned, probably with a change of title to *The Flexible Learning Handbook*, as the approach spans the uses of resource-based learning in training as well as education.

Race, P (1992) *53 Interesting Ways to Write Open Learning Materials* Technical and Educational Services, 37 Ravenswood Road, Bristol, BS6 6BW.
This book aims to provide 'manageable chunks' of suggestions for staff in further and higher education who wish to put together open learning packages.

Race, P (1992) *500 Tips for Students* Blackwell, Oxford.
This is in the same style as the present book, but written directly for students (and with some brilliant cartoons by a teenager). Like the present book, the emphasis is on active learning, and on helping students take increased responsibility for their own learning.

Ramsden, P (1992) *Learning to Teach in Higher Education* Routledge, London.
Essential reading for new and newish lecturers, linking theory to practice in valuable ways.

Rowntree, D (1992) *Exploring Open and Distance Learning* Kogan Page, London
A very thorough and professional account of the fields of open and distance learning, packed with learner-centred ideas, and with references to the rest of the literature in the field.

Rust, C (ed) (1991) *Changes of Course – Eight Case-Studies of Innovations in Higher Education Courses* SCED Publications, Gala House, Birmingham, B5 7RA.
It's always worth looking at 'how it can be done differently' when reflecting on our own approaches to teaching and learning. This SCED paper brings together eight accounts of innovatory approaches to both.

Rust, C (ed) (1990) *Teaching in Higher Education – An Induction Pack for New Lecturers* SCED Publications, Gala House, Birmingham, B5 7RA.
This pack collects together four articles to help new lecturers: 'Lecturing to large groups – a guide to doing it less – but better' (Lee Andresen), 'Small group teaching' (David Jaques), 'Using audio-visual aids creatively' (Kate Ashcroft, Graham Gibbs, David Jaques and Chris Rust) and 'An introduction to assessment (Graham Gibbs and Trevor Habeshaw). Collectively, the pack provides a rich variety of food for thought not only for new lecturers, but for experienced educators and trainers.

Rust, C (ed) (1992) *Teaching in Higher Education 2 – A Further Induction Pack for New Lecturers* SCED Publications, Gala House, Birmingham, B5 7RA.
This pack usefully collects together four papers suitable for new and experienced colleagues alike: 'Improving student learning' (Graham Gibbs), 'Supervising projects' (David Jaques), 'Being a personal tutor' (David Jaques) and 'Evaluating your teaching' (Diana Eastcott).

Index